Modern Homesteading

Rediscovering the American Dream

Wranglerstar PRODUCTION

First printing: October 2015

New Leaf Press is a division of the
New Leaf Publishing Group, Inc.

ISBN: 978-0-89221-737-3
Library of Congress Number: 2015951025

Cover Photo by Alan M. Thornton Productions
www.amtproductions.com

Design by Diana Bogardus

Unless otherwise noted, Scripture taken from the New King James Version (NKJV), copyright © 1982 by Thomas Nelson, Inc. Used by permission. All rights reserved.

Please consider requesting that a copy of this volume be purchased by your local library system.

Printed in the United States of America

Please visit our website for other great titles:
www.newleafpress.net

For information regarding author interviews, please contact the publicity department at (870) 438-5288

New Leaf Press
A Division of New Leaf Publishing Group
www.newleafpress.net

Learn timber framing tips, tools, and techniques with the Wranglerstar videos.

About This Book

Over the years, we have received numerous requests to reveal why we decided to move to the country and how we did it. In this book, we share some of our personal story. Each chapter is followed by a "how to" section, called "Wisdom from the Journey." It covers something we found out or wished we would have known before we embarked on our homesteading journey. The "Wisdom from the Journey" includes both practical tips and tools, as well as how this knowledge or lack of knowledge affected us or someone we know.

This is not intended to be an in-depth reference book, although we hope to save you from the mistakes we made and steer you in the right direction. We envisioned the book to be a companion to our YouTube channel, which can be found at Wranglerstar.com. We cover many of the topics in the book in greater detail on our channel. We do not purport to be experts at homesteading, but we work toward that goal.

"Homestead" is "the land and adjoining land occupied by a family" (Merriam-Webster.com). It further means "to acquire or occupy as a homestead." Historically, homesteading meant building and living on government land for a certain number of years in order to receive the property free of charge. Today, homesteading means something different; huge plots of land are no longer given away for free, electric or solar power is generally available, print material and media teach us skills we previously would have learned from our elders, and our survival is not incumbent on being able to grow, hunt, harvest, and preserve all of our own food. Modern homesteading is a process, not an event or place, different for each family. Most families will never achieve total self-sufficiency. For us, modern homesteading means making choices to improve the quality of the life of our family, while respecting the community and environment around us — not forsaking modern amenities, but learning old-fashioned skills and methodology and attempting self-sufficiency when conceivable (and, admittedly, convenient). To share our family's lifestyle, we use modern media, and the time it takes to produce videos eats up the time we might have spent doing something the slower, old-fashioned way. Modern homesteading balances use of contemporary technology to augment our homesteading lifestyle.

Why We Chose Modern Homesteading

While my wife wrote most of this book, you will find my views and suggestions throughout it. And because the question is so often asked, I want to first share why we chose to homestead.

For us, it was important for our family to separate itself from the chaos and distractions of an urban life. I'm not suggesting that homesteading should be used as an excuse to escape reality. The choice to homestead, whether it be 500 acres or five acres, should be about creating a sanctuary in a busy, overstimulated world. Our homesteading reality may look very different than yours; neither better nor worse.

The one thing we should all have in common is a desire to create and nurture a home environment that allows us, free from distraction, to build or cultivate a connection, a friendship with those we love, and for those of us that are Christians, a relationship with Christ. Whether you are Christian or not, the benefits transcend Christianity.

In our previous chaotic life, how could we tell people about Christ, the Prince of Peace, when we were still unsettled? Homesteading put us in a calming environment where we are less influenced by the attention-grabbing noise of our previous life. Even here, it can be a constant battle to protect peace and calmness. That being said, we feel like our shoulders are square, and our feet are firmly upon the right path.

The greatest benefit we, as a family, have received from making the decision to homestead is the ability to spend time together. I can only speak from my personal experience, but an additional benefit I received from making this decision can best be told by a personal revelation the second summer we were here. My wife and I were working in the garden. She was tending to some plants. I was on my hands and knees pulling weeds from the fence line. It dawned on me for the first time in my life that I was actually aware of my surroundings. I felt in tune with the changing of the seasons, the environment around me.

Up to this point, my entire life's focus and ambition had been to make money, build businesses, and acquire things. I had, in effect, limited myself to a type of tunnel vision — even though these things had been taking place around me, I had been completely unaware of them. In essence, I was coveting the things that were unimportant at the cost of those that were.

Although I have many hopes with this book, I do not know who you are, what your background is, or where you are coming from as you read this book. For me, it's not so important to have someone tell me how to do something — the important thing is to see them doing it. Talk is cheap, and actions speak louder than words. What I have done in life and portrayed in my videos are ideas and methods that are in no way unique to me. I am simply building on the accomplishments and courage of others who went before me.

This book and our YouTube channel work in concert to showcase many practical skills and ideas. What I hope they accomplish is to (1) provide you with hope and encouragement that you can change circumstances in your life, (2) teach you a skill that is tangible and of practical use, and (3) if nothing else, be entertaining to you, whether you are young or old.

—Cody, aka Wranglerstar
September 2015

(web link)

As you read our story, watch for these unique links. Videos have been created by Cody to enhance the content of each chapter of this book.

www.wranglerstar.com

Life Turned Upside Down

My husband, son, and I were in our van headed home after three days on the western slope of Glacier National Park. Unbeknownst to us then, those few days would radically change our lives. Twelve months earlier, I had read a book discussing the need to simplify life. "To simplify life," now a cliché to help you to clear the clutter from your closet, and, yet, at the time it represented something novel. The book suggested streamlining all aspects of your life in order to spend more time with your family. The author and his wife had quit their jobs, sold their home, and moved thousands of miles from their extended family — a drastic measure taken to keep their failing marriage and family together. The book further challenged readers to escape their chaotic lives to which our culture has grown accustomed. It presented practical concepts, not only lofty, theoretical goals. We heard the author speak at a lecture and spoke with him and his wife afterward. They extended an off-hand invitation to attend an event they were hosting at their remote, off-grid mountain home. We took them up on it and it was from that event that we were now driving away.

Twelve hours and three states away from home, we had a long drive to consider the people and lifestyle we had just experienced. Most of the attendees were conservative Christians beyond anything to which I had been exposed. All of the women wore long skirts — even when exercising

Traveling in our "adventure" van. We took out the seats and put in a bed, fridge, counter, and swivel seats.

or doing yard work. Dietary restrictions were strict and schedules firmly adhered to. Mainstream cultural experiences were extremely regulated. All toys were taken from the sandbox on the day of worship and it, as well as the swings, was off-limits to children. The children were homeschooled. The women definitely did not work outside of the home. These were not, and are not, our ways. I sensed my appearance pained them with my showy jewelry, painted toenails, shorts, and tank tops. Our son Jack wore printed tee shirts and shorts instead of plain, collared shirts and long pants. Very few times had I ever felt more out of place. However, they were kind, generous, and, astonishingly non-judgmental. We were not unwelcome, only decidedly different.

We appreciated our time with them and learned a great deal about dedication to family, having joy and laughter in life, and putting God first. They were not sticks in the mud. There was music, volleyball, camping, whitewater inner tubing, and playing tag — adults too. It was unadulterated fun. We desired many parts of it.

As my husband Cody and I discussed our trip at length, I was surprised to learn that the group setting and the roles people took appealed to him. It was reminiscent of positive experiences he had known in his childhood. While much differed, it felt normal to him, and comforting in its familiarity. While I watched and adapted to the odd social norms, he spent time learning about what it took to live off-grid and so remotely. He made hundreds of mental notes on solar panels, snow loads, gardening, pantry layout, logging, and adventure. Seeing the book's concepts in practice instead of just reading about them was more influential than we had imagined. During our drive home, we agreed we desired a life where we spent more time together, purposefully, as a family. Despite my quitting my job recently to stay home with Jack, Cody still worked a tremendous number of hours. Our marriage and family life felt the strain. We resolved to change many things, giving up our urban lifestyle.

We returned home motivated. We held no wish to be reclusive or harken back to bygone ways — however, we deemed change necessary. Our desire included moving farther out of the city to a truly remote location. Likewise, we were convinced I should educate Jack. We received some initial resistance from family and friends concerning our aspirations to relocate and to homeschool. Despite their uncertainty, they backed our struggle to achieve these goals. Although it is an ongoing evolution, we would now consider ourselves modern homesteaders.

The Power of YouTube

Approximately nine years ago, Cody began putting videos up on YouTube. He sold vehicle parts online and frequently explained, over the phone, how to install the same part repeatedly. Multiply this confusing task by the 1,500 parts he sold, the distinct ways people understand the same instructions, and varying mechanical skill levels, and Cody became an expert at giving step-by-step instructions in a clear manner. He quickly realized he could save countless hours if he performed the task once while filming, put the video up online, and directed purchasers to the website instead of answering numerous phone calls. With this revelation, our YouTube channel was born. What began as a car parts how-to site morphed into a do-it-yourself channel of another flavor. Our channel name, Wranglerstar, reveals our history — "Wrangler" from Jeep parts and "Star" from a location meaning a great deal to us.

Because the YouTube community was so small back then, little concern was given to privacy issues, such as where we lived, or the name of our son. Once you share some things, you simply cannot take them back. As viewers became familiar with us, they requested we increase the number of videos of more mundane activities, such as rescuing Morris the cat from a tree, setting off water bottle rockets with an air compressor, or

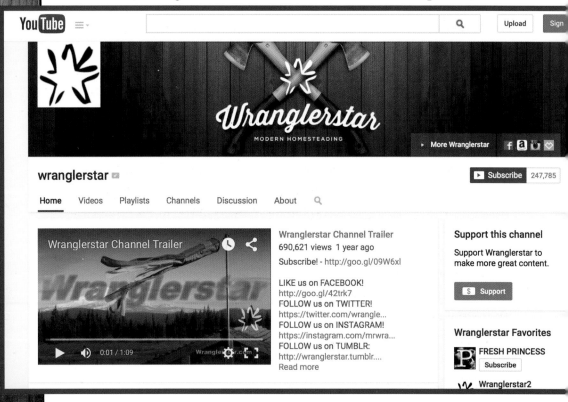

Jack giggling madly while riding his little electric quad, pulling Cody in wild fashion through the shop on a dolly (a small platform on wheels used for moving heavy objects). Never did we anticipate our daily lives would be of interest to anyone but ourselves.

Early on, Cody added some gear review videos and political commentary, and has always conducted Bible studies. He received positive feedback and his number of subscribers began to accumulate. A wildly popular YouTuber featured one of Cody's videos, back in the days when you could show someone else's video on your own channel. We were at a barbecue when Cody starting getting email notifications his subscriber base was rapidly multiplying. Without that exposure, our channel may never have grown to the size it is today.

The mixture of instructional how-to videos, online Bible study, and everyday-life videos taught Cody how to highlight the necessary information with enjoyable moments. He was forced to answer questions, discuss difficult topics, and highlight the beauty of commonplace occurrences. Feedback taught him what topics viewers appreciated or disdained. In the beginning, he had no idea how to edit—shooting all videos in one take, which often meant 10 to 15 takes to get it perfect, or "close enough." He believed producing videos would be so much easier if he could only splice two video segments together. Back then, consumer-level video editing software was not readily available like it is today. As the subscriber base increased, it put demands on Cody to up his game to make higher quality, better content videos. He started to pay closer attention to movies and videos, becoming a student of transitions and jump cuts. He taught himself to edit using a free downloaded version of Corel®.

As he sought to educate others, he too has been educated. When our bulldozer would stop running, we appreciated how bulldozer experts emerged with useful tips and explanations of complex mechanical fixes. We saved a tremendous amount of time, effort, and money because of these knowledgeable and experienced viewers. To those viewers — keep those comments coming! We love learning. Of course, there were "experts" who had never picked up a tool, much less touched a bulldozer. Those types of self-proclaimed "experts," while not the norm, were, and continue to be, frustrating. They criticize our decisions and us more than anyone else does. On the other hand, those with genuine wisdom tend to be exceedingly gracious, and valued.

With our move to the off-grid location, the number of videos Cody produced increased dramatically. Developing an off-grid site was unusual and interesting. Subscribers poured in. The quality of the videos from that period was low, in part because of the lack of time to devote to

This is reality. We lack the polish and staged drama of television actors.... We openly show our successes and failures.

editing and a horrific Internet connection. We had other jobs at hand. Investment in a quality camera and editing software also were not paramount for us. Cody purchased a flip camera for $100 and continued to use Corel®'s basic editing software, which sold for under $50. Many of those videos are no longer available, as YouTube changed music copyright policies, forcing us to delete them. Since the era of the off-grid property, our video and editing equipment has been upgraded. Cody purchased a used Apple laptop, and still uses consumer-level editing software. He bought a refurbished Cannon video camera and an iPhone®. He invests little in cameras because he exposes them to terrible weather from constant outdoor filming — they career out of trees, and tripods fall over. Because of subscriber demands, he now attempts to upload a video daily. His hours remain much longer than Jack and I prefer, but he works from home, so we can, and do, interrupt him frequently. Responding to viewer comments and emails requires more hours than occupy a day. Please forgive him if he does not answer yours. Cody makes a valiant attempt, but falls short. However, the comments and emails compel us to continue to videotape our everyday occurrences.

Somehow, our struggles and successes at our off-grid property became a bit of a poor man's reality TV show. People tuned in regularly. When the set changed from off-grid to our present-day homestead, the viewers came along. We lack the polish and staged drama of television actors, but people tell us they prefer that. When we work outdoors, our clothes show dirt and stains, our hair remains uncombed, our faces reveal no make-up, and dialogue comes naturally. We lack the expensive tools and equipment of the professionals. People relate to us. We claim no more strength, wealth, or intelligence than the average viewer does. As one subscriber told us, "I like that you aren't Martha Stewarts, where everything is perfect, placed somewhere for a reason, and expensive. Watching her can make you struggle with feelings of inadequacy." We openly show our successes and failures. Jack summed it up nicely one time: "This is reality." I imagine that is why people watch. It is strange to share our life so publicly. It was not our intent.

Somehow, a ministry has emerged from ax handles, composting, and hard work. Our viewers remind us daily that we are blessed to have this family, home, and adventure. I used to believe people watched us because we also readily admit to believing in God. In reality, that is the most controversial topic on our channel. Viewers tend to either love or hate the mention of our beliefs. Interestingly, this division cannot be drawn between Christians and non-Christians. Some atheists are our strongest supporters. Some Christians are our biggest critics.

Honestly, I approach our YouTube channel with hesitation, because of the weight of responsibility it brings. I toiled diligently at its creation, endured much to ensure its success, and have been of support to Cody in his efforts. I enjoy the fruits of this labor, but like many good things, I sometimes wonder if I am up to the task. I do not shirk hard work or difficult situations, but we all bear different types of responsibility better than other types. Perhaps I consider the channel too seriously, but the messages we receive tell us we are involved in a ministry, whether we intended it or not. That makes me nervous. I know God uses the least, but I feel a little bit too least even for Him sometimes. I often want to ask Him if He is sure about His choice. I do not mean to sound too casual or disrespectful, but I know He wants to hear my fears and struggles. When I pray, God tells me He will use both Cody and me if we let Him. I find when I follow His lead, something better than I might imagine generally emerges.

Tree planting party with subscribers and friends

An example involves our open houses at the homestead. A number of times each year, we invite subscribers to play, labor, and fellowship on our property. Once a year we invite them to camp from three to five days. I always ask people why they come. Why do people drive long distances to camp on hard ground and work all day with strangers? One couple from California replied, "We wanted to see what you and Cody were really like. What are people like who trust enough to open their home and property to one hundred complete strangers?" Put that way, I understood how crazy we might seem. I answered that, despite my reluctance, God had asked us to invite viewers, so we did. Despite my insecurities, I choose to share what I treasure. By the time the couple left, they understood why we continue to host, without any need for further explanation. Despite all of our differences in background, skill level, and ideology, a harmony emerges as people work and socialize together.

Cody recently posted a video in which he said we would be planting trees. He did not request any help and yet I received over half a dozen emails from previous open house attendees asking if they may come and plant. Clearly, they do not desire to come because planting one thousand conifers on their day off excites them. They come because of the camaraderie and satisfaction from simple work. People yearn for these types of real experiences, challenging their bodies, their strength, and accomplishing teamwork. This is not our doing. We simply open our gate to allow it to happen here.

Years ago, we benefitted when people opened their homes to us and wrote books on homesteading. We likely would not have traded in our urban lifestyle for a simpler, rural way of life had it not been for them. Because of this, we feel an obligation to share our homesteading journey too. We do not aspire for others to live a life similar to ours, but to forge ahead with their own dreams and implement the changes they want in their lives. The medium to share our story simply happens to be videos. Through YouTube we can dialogue with others; ask, answer, suggest, and learn. This channel has provided a useful way to interact between creators and subscribers.

Questions abound about how we support ourselves on the homestead. YouTube began in 2005, and in 2007, launched its revenue-sharing Partner Program. After a year of uploading videos, YouTube invited us to join its Partner Program. We were thrilled with the $30 paychecks we received each month. Today we receive income from both the advertisements playing prior to our videos and for sales made through our online streams. After eight years of making videos, the checks only recently amounted to enough for us to make videos fulltime. At first, I felt guilty for receiving a paycheck for making videos. I then realized that, combined, we spend well over 90 hours a week on videoing, editing, production, commenting, emailing, and bookkeeping. I could find no reason not to receive compensation for the work we do.

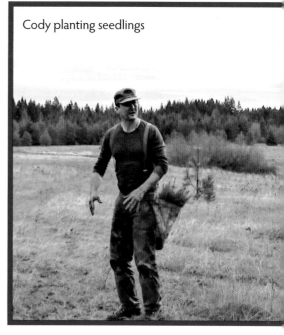

Cody planting seedlings

Cody also contracts on wildland fires to supplement our income. We are not rich; we still cannot afford to remodel our house, buy a tractor, or visit my brother and his family who live overseas, and whom we miss terribly. We budget strictly, purchase most of our clothes at thrift stores, and buy used when possible. I am not complaining, only answering a frequent question. Together, we prioritized this lifestyle over other choices. I am glad we did, and yes, we have started to save for part of the remodel and a trip. The tractor will have to wait.

In the beginning, I wanted absolutely no part of the YouTube channel. Indeed, it brought up concerns about time consumed and private information revealed. Perhaps because I am a woman, but sharing personal information with a stranger was the antithesis of all the safety messages

I had heard over the years. So please refer to our mountain as Mt. Fuji, which it is not. Let people know we live in Colorado, which we do not. We understand with over one thousand videos, people gain an intimate knowledge of our family. After so much exposure, we cannot fake who we are. On the flip side, we lack any information about the majority of people we meet. It is strange, really. We are blessed to meet so many wonderful people whom we suspect could be close friends if the situation were normal. But it is not. They know us, but we do not know them. There can be very strong expectations, which can be tricky to manage. Often we can only enjoy a few minutes or hours with someone. People stop by uninvited, creating awkward moments both for them and for us. When I am home alone, and a strange man comes through our gate, I am not elated, as you can understand. We love invited guests though! Plus, our house gets messy, our schedules are full, and that is why we hold the open houses.

I am a gifted listener, but a reluctant storyteller. I avoid public speaking. With no hesitation, I stand up to provide information I know or my opinion in front of a small crowd, but do not ask me to prepare and deliver a speech to ten of my closest friends. This disdain for speaking allowed me to escape appearing in Cody's videos for the first five years or so. Thus, I kept my anonymity. Cody laughed when I suggested penning this book as Mrs. Cody. While he was pleased I am proud to be his wife, he considers me a bit ridiculous. Nonetheless, to keep the mystery alive, please do not reveal my first or maiden name; I prefer to be called Mrs. Wranglerstar.

Despite my reluctance, the pressure to participate in videos was real. Although initially successful in shying away from the spotlight, Cody convinced me the success of the channel relied upon contributions from the entire family, and not just off-screen. When I saw how much Cody despised working with Jeep parts, and how difficult it was for his body, it proved impossible to say no. Honestly, he had no interest in Jeeps or parts sales, but diligently ran the business for over a decade because it provided a means for me to stay home with Jack. The hours were long, the work dirty and taxing, and all of his shops were regularly bitterly cold or miserably hot. The wrenching of parts, at awkward positions, caused his back and limbs to suffer ongoing pain. Every morning he struggled out of bed. Many mornings I had to help him out of bed. Visits to the chiropractor were frequent. I would do anything to alleviate his suffering, even appearing in videos.

In early 2015, we were able to shut down our online Jeep parts store. Skills and livelihood were gathered there, a blessing for certain, but what a relief. As Cody worked more on videos and less on part sales, his pain subsided. I daresay a complete recovery occurred. And this is why we run a YouTube channel called Wranglerstar.

https://goo.gl/FVOv8n

Our Wranglerstar family

Acquiring Skills and Some Stories

"Where did you acquire your homesteading skills?" "What jobs and experiences taught you those skills? "Where do I get those skills?" These three questions make our list of most frequently requested information. As you determine whether urban homesteading or a transition to rural life is right for you, make sure you take advantage of the opportunities right before you. Skills we acquired along the way are relevant today. There are different times in life where you gain unique and useful skills. Keep in mind that even if you acquire certain skills, nothing requires you to do everything on your own. While there is pride in running a self-sufficient homestead, some tasks you enjoy more than others. Some periods allow you more (or less) time to do projects. Learn to can jam and jelly, make yogurt, mill your wood, butcher your meat, tend to your beehive, dip your own candles, prune your fruit trees, raise goats and cows, dig your well, but do not feel obligated to do all of them all of the time. While I bake most of our bread, convenience dictates that purchasing loaves happens. Cody loves to mill his own lumber, but sometimes Home Depot® is a much quicker route.

We live in an era where we can do many things ourselves, but the obligation to do so in order to survive is not as real. Many activities are things families can do together, both to learn and to enjoy time together. Many of the skills you gain might be unique and interesting, but leave you wondering if they are really part of the lifestyle you are trying to create. Yes, no matter what you learn, there will be an application. Get out of the books. Get off YouTube (not completely). If you want to learn homesteading skills, you must get dirty. As much as you read about gardening, you need to get soil under your fingernails to understand. If you want to sharpen a knife, you cannot just watch a YouTube video; you need to get your knives out. Some homesteading skills are more useful than others. No one becomes an expert at all of them.

Learning by Doing

Where should you acquire your skills? Everywhere. Do what you find interesting or useful. Go to school, take a class, travel, work. Learn. Learn about things you cannot begin to fathom are interesting. Fly-fishing? "Hand me a rod." Pressure canning? "I will peel the potatoes." Photography? "Show me which button to push." Want to travel to Romania? "Book my ticket." You may not love the activity or the experience, but you may be able to apply newly acquired skills elsewhere at a later date. A love of learning the Greek language may allow you to travel to Greece as a translator where you do volunteer work and learn to fish, which allows you to buy a boat and labor as a fisherman, which allows you to save for and purchase a piece of property. One thing really does lead to another. I do not speak Greek, but traveled to Greece as a translator (and the Czech Republic the same year) because I speak Swedish and English. The Greek (and Czech) spoke English and I translated into Swedish. Strange skill, great trips.

Even with the most mundane job, you can learn something new. Sometimes you simply learn you really do not want to work in that field of employment. We all worked jobs we are glad to be done with. Sometimes they are right for one part of your life, but not another. Cody pressed buttons in an assembly line, fixed small engines, ran heavy equipment, roofed, framed, poured concrete, laid pipe, and tore apart Jeeps.

When Cody's granddad retired, he hired on as a mechanic on a fleet of trucks for a sanitation equipment company, where he helped Cody get a job for a few summers. Cody put brand new porta-potties together half the time and the other half, well, he cleaned. The experience helped him realize what he did not want to do for a living.

He says, "I didn't exactly enjoy many of my jobs and felt like I was not living up to my potential." He wanted to

Cody brings intensity and a willingness to teach others what he has learned in the YouTube videos.

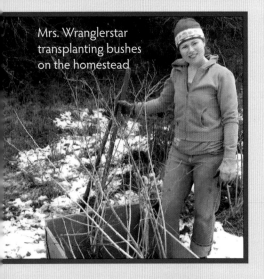

Mrs. Wranglerstar transplanting bushes on the homestead

Mrs. Wranglerstar finishing the rugged 90 km Vasaloppet cross country ski race in Sweden

A young Cody catches some air while skiing

do something else; the jobs were not a good fit for him. Looking back, he believes "it was part of God's plan. I needed these skills and his abilities later. If I had not learned them at a young age, I may never have learned them. Every job has directly played into homesteading."

As an onsite construction superintendent for an international construction company building stores in commercial spaces, where deadlines were strict, Cody learned to finish projects quickly and efficiently and how to manage large groups of people, regardless of obstacles and setbacks, improvising as necessary. When we were first married, he was contacted by a firm who wanted him to return to building stores. The pay was good. I was impressed. He was flattered. We considered it for half a day, but his being gone about ten months per year living in hotels seemed like a lonely alternative for both of us.

During my college and graduate school years, I slopped plates in the dish room at a cafeteria, worked in the fields, did custodial work, waited tables, sold furniture, and taught English. One of my motivations was to graduate with as little debt as possible, which enabled me to be pickier, later, when choosing employment. I could move where I wanted and choose a lower-paying job because I was not tied to the burden of student loan debt the size of a mortgage. All of our jobs served a purpose at the time. They provided income and taught us skills. For the young reader, longing to be on your own land, that job you disdain might not be lost time but perhaps building skills you will need later — skills to allow you to do what you want to do. Roofing for someone else and roofing your very own dream home is the same job, but feels very different.

The Value of Hard Work

Our parents worked hard and anticipated we do the same. Chores were plentiful. Expectations were set. There was no sitting around watching television or playing video games all day. Cody's dad and granddad shared construction and mechanical skills with him. My mom taught me fundamental kitchen skills. Our parents showed us there was nothing to stop us from achieving our dreams or trying something new. Neither set of parents let fear of failure hinder them in business ventures or acquiring new skills. We both inherited this can-do attitude. After a hard day of physical labor, we have been known to comment we certainly could not have married somebody lazy or afraid of risk. Clearly, hard work has helped us be able to purchase the homestead and complete some of its many, many projects. To good and to ill, there is a bit of workaholic in both of us. *"I went by the field of the lazy man, and by the vineyard of the man devoid of understanding; and there it was, all overgrown with thorns; its surface was covered with nettles; its stone wall was broken down. When I saw it, I considered it well; I looked on it and received instruction: a little sleep, a little slumber, a little folding of the hands to rest; so shall your poverty come like a prowler, and your need like an armed man* (Proverbs 24:30–34).

Our parents worked hard and anticipated we do the same.

It Takes Time

You will notice in our homesteading story that there are no stories of collecting eggs from the chicken coop or putting the cows in the pasture. We eat local eggs, drink local raw milk and use it to make cheese and yogurt, and delight in pasture-raised beef (from right next door) but have not yet committed to animal husbandry. Rome was not built in a day, and neither is our homestead. We add and delete forest and farm chores as our time and desires enable us. Jack says he wants chickens, but balks when we tell him he has to care for them. The poor boy does not hurt for chores. I tell Cody not to take down all of the fencing because of our future Dexter cows, goats, lambs, and little pigs. Then I recall that with animals you must choose the correct type, construct a place to put them, erect fencing strong enough to enclose them, keep your pastures in excellent shape and avoid overgrazing them, buy extra hay and silage if necessary, pay vet costs, consider reproduction (or not and wish you had), milk, shear, and then butcher your new "pets." After writing this, I know why we house our fifth wheel in our big barn instead of animals. I am with Jack — I balk at the thought of more to do on a daily basis. The dream of complete self-sufficiency and "doing it all" does not always couple with the time constraints of daily living.

Sometimes while waiting on things to come together you have to make do with what you can find. We have all heard the stories of getting job offers in the strangest situations. And it is true. Ask questions. Make yourself available to opportunities. Cody has had many jobs and rarely filled out an application. Likewise, I bought a bike, was polite, and got offered, and accepted, a job before I left the store. I volunteered a few times at a school and was eventually offered a position when one opened up. I attended a ski swap and received a job offer without swapping any skis. I will tell you about it after sharing Cody's experience in Wildland Firefighting.

Wildland Fire Management

In the 1990s, Cody decided a career in firefighting would suit him. He

Cody working a fire

attended night school after work at a community college to obtain his certification as an EMT/paramedic, which would enable him to apply to numerous fire academies. During that time, he spent many hours on an ambulance in an urban setting where he encountered gunshot wounds, domestic violence incidents, car accidents, drug overdoses, and general illnesses. This bolstered his belief that firefighting would be more to his

Cody with
home-built
fire engine

liking. Upon completion, he applied to departments, ultimately deciding upon a fire academy in Colorado. While there, he not only completed his basic requirements, but took coursework to become a hazardous material technician and firefighting engineer. Because his department covered a section of Interstate 70 in the mountains, he saw his fair share of gruesome and heartbreaking accidents. He also fought fires on wildland crews in the Rockies, figuring out that he enjoyed fighting wildland fires more than structural fires. When he chose to leave that department to return to his beloved Pacific Northwest, he began fixing, then parting Jeeps, in order to pay the bills until he could get on with another fire department. Things quickly changed as a wife, home, and baby kept him with his stable Jeep business.

Years later, he has been able to rekindle his interest by joining a local volunteer fire department. He now responds to structural and wildland fires, as well as car accidents and other needs. The station closest to us had been closed because no volunteer lived close enough to staff it. Cody now has his "own" station where he keeps "his" fire rig. He stores his gear in his pickup in case he needs to respond at a moment's notice. While there are distinct boundaries between the fire districts, everyone helps each other out.

One day Cody responded to a rollover vehicle crash seven or eight miles from our home. He took his personal medical kit and pickup, not bothering to get the fire station rig, which would have delayed him

25 to 30 minutes. He arrived at least 15 minutes before anyone else, even though it was not even in his district. The man eventually needed to be life-flighted out. The arriving medic had been trained, but had not experienced working with such injury before. Despite his lapsed paramedic credentials, Cody was able to walk and talk the terrified medic through the necessary steps to assist the grievously injured man. Once you learn skills, they might get rusty but you do not lose them.

In addition to Cody's volunteer work, he has been completing course-work for various levels of national wildland firefighting certification. While he loves the volunteer work, someone has to pay the bills. Each level of certification requires coursework in addition to actual "task" work that must be completed while actively fighting wildland fires. This ensures that wildland firefighters possess both head and practical knowledge when dealing with dangerous situations or directing others under them. He directly contacts federal and state agencies if he sees they are offering a class he is interested in or needs. While he takes mandatory coursework to move up in certification, he also takes classes on topics such as logging or engine safety. He fulfills his duty with a contractor who holds higher certification than he holds and can "take him under his wing." Cody can be gone for extended periods of time taking courses or fighting wildland fires. So if video quality decreases, you know who is manning the YouTube "station" while he is gone. Remember — I am just a volunteer!

Sled Dogs

When I was about 25, I spoke at length with a dog musher at a ski swap about traveling to Canada and Northern Minnesota on a ten-day winter camping, cross-country skiing and dog-sledding trip while in college. Minus 40 degrees at the time of the trip, I returned with frostbite on my skin. I still suffer the effects, but it does not diminish my love of winter, although I now dress with extreme care. One day, despite warnings, a group member momentarily stepped off the sled and fell through the ice. Even at that cold temperature, the current in the river kept the ice thin. A blazing fire was made quickly, dry clothes pulled from stuffed packs, and a shivering young man revived. The danger was real. Not accustomed to the rigors of cold or so much physical exertion from running beside the sled and cross-country skiing for hours on end, people moved with exhaustion. We grabbed the packs of those too tired and skied ahead with heavier loads to set up camp for those behind us. We burned through calories at an astonishing rate, melting sticks of butter into everything we ate. At the end of the trip, awards were given, and I received a chocolate turkey for my good attitude and putting up with a heavily male-dominated trip. I was the sole female with over 20 college-aged males, a handful of male guides, and two very protective male professors.

During the conversation with the musher we exchanged names. Later that week I received a phone call from him offering me a job as his dog handler and assistant musher. Both flattered and alarmed, I wavered in my response. To be clear, he was older, had a ten-year-old daughter who lived with him, and nothing felt inappropriate. Despite knowing little of dogs or mushing, I moved to the countryside with him and his two male mushers. His daughter and I shared a room and bunk-beds. Much to the

Back when Mrs. Wranglerstar learned to be a dogsledder

delight of the males in the dwelling, I spent countless evenings teaching the musher's daughter how to cook, which was interesting, because she was legally blind. In exchange, she taught me about dogs, at which she was already an expert.

In Training

We trained dogs on both snow and dry land. On snow, we used sleds in tandem with anywhere from 10 to 17 dogs at a time. It was majestic, flying along on trails, through forested woods, up on the mountain. While typically very focused and running steadily, if the dogs became tangled in the rope, danger could erupt. Imagine a pile of muscular, adrenalin-filled dogs ensnared in rope, piling on top of each other, and trying to free themselves. We would quickly throw the sleds on their sides to stop forward momentum, anchor the snow hooks, wade through deep snow and attempt to pull them apart. Sometimes it was best to pull the lead dogs ahead to straighten out the rope, always watching to make sure the rope did not choke a dog or wrap around a limb. Once calmed, we began again. On land, we followed behind the dogs in a beaten-up,

well-worn sedan with the top cut off. Attractive, no. Useful, yes. The setup was perfect for building muscle and tiring out the dogs.

The dog yard was a collection of plastic dog houses and retired wire spools, holes cut in the sides, for the dogs to find protection. Each dog was on a rope attached to a stake in the ground. Most dogs could reach one another to play but kept far enough apart not to become twisted. There were a few kennels for the dogs that rubbed their necks raw if attached to a stake. Missy was a smart dog that could unhook her collar, and was repeatedly found roaming among the other dogs, tails wagging. Because the musher gave rides to tourists, dogs had to be friendly and trustworthy, so that any toddler could pet them roughly without worry. The dogs were watered, fed, and cleaned up after at least twice a day. We scooped enormous masses of poop. One hundred dogs. It added up rapidly. Each dog was petted profusely, talked to, and loved on. Surprisingly, even with that many dogs, it was always quiet, until a human started scooping food or pulling out harnesses and ropes indicating it was time to run. These dogs loved to run — ached, thrilled, and yearned to run. When they were not chosen, they evidenced their disappointment.

Race to the Finish

The musher ran a concession on the mountain, which paid for his sledding and dog addiction, and occasionally raced in local events. However, he felt the itch to race at the elite level again. I had been hired to help train and handle the racing dogs with the owner, while three young men worked the concession. Sled dog racing can be broken into three categories: sprint, mid-distance, and long-distance. Mid-distance is generally anywhere from 100 to 300 miles, either continuous or stage races (split up into numerous days). The high-stakes race he competed in was a stage-stop race of roughly 400 miles in the Rocky Mountains.

We started training the prospective racing team with 25 dogs. Some were too slow to be chosen. Others were too inconsistent, pulling hard

one day and not at all the next. Missy and Murphy proved to be reliable, effective lead dogs, in the front, together, directing the team. Chris was Murphy's litter mate and both could have passed for black labs. Murphy craved human affection, clearly desiring to be a lap dog, while Chris was so timid it was painful. He was one of the dogs that occupied a kennel, was strong, loved to run, and pulled hard, making him a perfect wheel dog. He endured Romeo, the other wheel dog. Romeo fit his name, strong and charming, but a bit daft. Gus was young, nearly too young to make the team, but ran with exuberance and speed, making the cut to the top 18 dogs. Gus's problem was he refused to eat, preferring to play, run, or sleep. The increased volume of running and pulling put him at a worrisome weight. To fatten up dogs, we melted enormous kettles of chicken fat to add to selected dogs' food. Sponsors provided dog food, frozen chicken and meat, and chicken fat. I drove my sedan to pick up five-gallon buckets of fat, lining the trunk of my car with newspapers and tarps, hoping nothing spilled.

Preparing to race included not only training the dogs, but also training ourselves. Because I ran alongside the sled whenever we went uphill, manhandled the dogs, and hauled gear, I exercised a great deal. I was in marathon shape with bulging biceps by the end of the sledding season. Preparing gear and food included packing some 500 pounds of frozen chicken and 250 pounds of frozen beef for the dogs, plus harnesses, ropes, sleds, and the dogs themselves, not to mention overnight winter camping equipment for the musher. Each morning of the race, I readied the sled and dogs and got the musher on his way. I then cared for the other dogs, loaded up the already overloaded truck, and drove on icy roads up steep mountain passes. His young daughter along and in my charge, we would arrive at our next race stop, setting up for when the sled came in. The musher and dogs arrived hungry, tired, and thirsty. Occasionally, a dog would be riding in the sled, too tired or injured to continue. Dogs were staked out, food and water provided, booties taken off and paws checked. Damage to the sled was repaired and runners waxed. Rope and harnesses were checked and swapped out if necessary. It was a busy time, and exhilarating. The season ended too quickly.

Applied Skills

How does my time with sled dogs associate with homesteading? Skills and hard work. Skills I did not even know I picked up are used on the homestead. Knot-tying, securing large loads, dressing properly in inclement conditions, driving overloaded vehicles, not panicking in dangerous situations, and the list goes on. Hard work — well, homesteading demands it.

Whatever jobs you may find yourself doing, do them well and with a good attitude. You will learn things, be presented with unanticipated opportunities, and have pride in your work and yourself. Integrity is what you do when no one is watching. You may not reap the rewards immediately but they will come. *". . . and in the labor which you perform under the sun. Whatever your hand finds to do, do it with your might…"* (Ecclesiastes 9:9–10).

https://goo.gl/uV4j0y

Wranglerstar
homesteading
showcases family
teamwork.

Everything to the Glory of God

I always feel a sense of gratitude for the ability God has given me to create things. There's nothing like building something with your own hands and creating something that's real. I look forward to the day when I can perfect my skills in eternity. Maybe I'll be able to create a house or a room that is suitable to invite the Lord to spend the evening.

When I'm timber framing or doing other tasks on the homestead, it can sometimes seem like I'm being over meticulous with trying to make my timbers as straight and flat as possible. Or taking extra time to do a job right. It's easy to do things halfway, but I realize that God calls us to do everything to His glory, which involves being excellent wherever you are and with whatever you're doing (1 Corinthians 10:31).

If you are faithful in little things, you will be faithful in large ones. But if you are dishonest in little things, you won't be honest with greater responsibilities (Luke 16:10 NLT).

Making videos for the channel takes a lot of effort. It takes a lot of creativity and thought. And sometimes I feel uninspired or that I don't have much to offer. There have been times where a television producer wants to send film crews out for various projects, and I tell them all the

same thing. The day to day work of homesteading isn't very intriguing. There's a lot going on but as I do those things I am thinking "is this interesting" or "do I want to bore someone with the things that are going on"? It may just be simple maintenance or repair. Or it may be getting ready for a change in seasons – from fall to winter or winter to spring. It can be big projects or just little things.

We all have to work, but what does the way we do that work say about us as a person? We should all strive to do our tasks perfectly every time, whether we work for someone else or on our own homestead. It's not always easy but you have to start somewhere – personally and professionally. Sometimes it means changing our mindset – doing something we haven't done before or not being afraid to try. And focusing on who and what really matters in what we do.

I take this seriously when it comes to my role as a father. Fathers can instill character, integrity, and good attitudes, but there's a conscious effort throughout society to undermine the role of the father. To solve this, we have to start at home.

Fatherhood is important because it's the foundation of society. Fathers should be gentle, meek, and honest, but shouldn't be pushovers. They have to stand up for what's right against injustices, but they should never lord over the family or the home. They should be priests of the home, educating the family spiritually, and lead by example.

And these words which I command you today shall be in your heart. You shall teach them diligently to your children, and shall talk of them when you sit in your house, when you walk by the way, when you lie down, and when you rise up (Deuteronomy 6:6-7).

It's easy not to take fatherhood seriously or to truly understand its importance, but we have to remember that everything we do, large and small, at work or in our home, should be for God's glory. I might never get things as perfect as I would like them to be, but that doesn't mean that I shouldn't strive for perfection. Whether it's timber framing or being a father, I hope to use my skills every day to honor God.

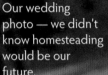

2. Our Beginning

It was autumn, over a decade ago, and I invited a bunch of friends over for a barbecue. A short time before, I had moved back to the Pacific Northwest after having been gone for three years, completing my graduate degree. My parents were visiting from the Midwest. I had originally moved to Portland, Oregon, seven years earlier. My parents liked meeting up with my old friends so I was hosting a party. My dad went to a nearby store to buy last-minute groceries. My mom and I prepped food and straightened up the yard and tiny duplex I rented. Some of my best friends called and asked if they could bring another friend who recently moved back to the area. "Sure." Later, he arrived, alone, before my friends. My dad returned, carrying more than

Our wedding photo — we didn't know homesteading would be our future.

the hot dogs he had gone to purchase. In tow, he carried a small television set, as I neglected to own one, and he needed one. My home-state college football team was playing later, and for him, it was imperative to watch them win.

The Unlikely Couple

Later, the party started and in walked a handsome man with jet-black hair, deeply tanned skin, a lean, muscular frame, and with a swagger to boot. "That is a whole lot of attitude," I thought unfavorably. I introduced myself and quickly left this man's presence as soon as could be deemed polite. After the party, my mom relayed she had engaged in a

The beauty of Portland in autumn

wonderful conversation with "that long fellow" and asked what I thought of him. She grew up in Sweden, and despite living here for over 45 years, still speaks with a strong accent and mixes up words in an endearing manner. I told her I took an immediate dislike to "that long fellow" and hoped not to see him again.

Cody says he knows nothing about being handsome, or having a swagger, but in the past, he tended to hold ill-gotten, preconceived notions regarding people with more education than him. Our mutual friends had described me and he suspected I would be smug before even meeting me, so our initial encounter reflected that. Curiously, he overlooked associating my educational level with my parents upon meeting them. Growing up he had not known many foreigners or people who traveled abroad, and always found it fascinating to speak with them. He had never met anyone from Sweden and found my mother "delightful, engaging, and interesting."

The following week, the friends who invited him warned me he would be at their gathering. I could not understand what they saw in him, and avoided him. I noticed he also avoided me. At one point, we were forced into conversation and it was awkward at best. He behaved courteously and upheld his end of the small talk, but we parted the instant we were able. Despite his bias, he thought I possessed an infectious laugh, and left with a more favorable impression of me than before. Similarly, I enjoyed listening to him speak warmly and lovingly about his granddad.

The following week, our mutual friends were headed to his apartment for a potluck. For some reason, he told them to invite me. My friends did, but also brought six gorgeous, blonde co-workers in order to set Cody up. Six o'clock arrived and I showed up with a roasted chicken. I learned three things that evening. First, the potluck had been changed to seven o'clock. Second, he preferred redheads to blondes. Third, the way to a man's heart really is through his belly. And so began things with Cody.

We were, however, an unlikely couple. We grew up in vastly dissimilar families with divergent ideas regarding education, free time, society, and religion. We would hardly make polite dinner conversationalists. While we did not argue much, we looked at each other quizzically quite often, trying to figure out how each other's brains functioned. Some things that were a given in my family were not expectations or the norm for Cody, and vice versa.

Cody was born into a tight-knit church community where most people married young, were discouraged from pursuing higher education, immediately began working in a hands-on profession upon graduation, and stuck around close to home. Cody even grew up in the house his grandparents built; they dug out the basement by hand. His parents slowly added on to enlarge the diminutive structure, even building the window frames by hand from recycled glass. Everyone in the family seemed to be born with gifted hands — for mechanics, construction, sewing, and painting, to name a few. Cody and his sister were oddities in their community, traveling, moving around, and not marrying right out of high school. When I met him, he was in his thirties, and I think his mother worried he would never marry.

I grew up in a family that valued higher education, accepted women marrying later, and moved far away from both sides of the family. My mom even immigrated to the United States to marry a Yankee. In our leisure, we read, visited museums, cooked, and ran. Both my brother and I studied and worked abroad. Not so surprisingly, but much to my parents' chagrin, I followed their lead and moved approximately two thousand miles away from home, to the West Coast.

When Cody and I met we had both recently moved back to Portland after leaving for a few years. A short time before, Cody had quit his job as a structural/wildland firefighter medic, while I had completed graduate school. We fell madly in love, spent all of our available time together, and talked of marriage. Eventually, I grew tired of talk. A year after we started dating, I questioned Cody's sincerity about marriage. I explained I was getting older, wanted children and a family, and was a "reasonable catch," so though it would be sad, I needed to know if I should "move on." He sat flabbergasted, stunned, and proclaimed his undying love for me. Five months later, we married.

City Folks

While we were engaged, we bought a fixer-upper of a house, supposing an urban lifestyle would continue to be perfect for us. It was located in a mediocre neighborhood at best, and that may be generous. Every evening after work we would gut the old farmhouse in an attempt to bring back the appeal stolen by previous owners. Several "remuddles" had taken place. We chose this house because it was a deal and oozed with old

house "charm." Jokingly, Cody says, "Hanging out with the Portland crowd, I got bamboozled into a romanticism to live in a drafty, one hundred-year-old, crooked house. People say they do not make them like they used to and thank goodness for that."

Our fixer-upper in Portland

I quickly learned Cody possessed skills, useful skills. His father had been a contractor, and his granddad a mechanic, and both passed on tricks of their trade. Additionally, Cody had owned an excavating company, and later been an onsite project manager for a commercial general contractor specializing in core and shell projects (building stores in commercial spaces). Couple all of that together with some how-to books from a hardware store and Cody was practically unstoppable.

Our fixer-upper still needs fixin'.

This "deal" had no driveway or garage or shed, despite the fact my husband loves to work with his hands. He is a tool man. An engine and wood man. Usually filthy, befitting of slipcovers on the couch, type of man. The smell of oil and sap always upon him (although he cleans up well). This house had no shop for him. Not even a concrete pad upon which to tinker. A grungy, dank basement with low ceilings for a very tall man.

We worked on this house as a labor of love while both maintaining full-time employment. I had a corporate job earning a lucrative salary. Cody had an entrepreneurial spirit and endeavored to start an online business. We each still rented our own places while planning our wedding. After our regular workday, we rushed to the house to renew that which was old. To restore charm. To strip away the ugly added by so many. We toiled until our bones ached and the hours were late. We would say goodnight and part company.

Cody's Jeep arrived outside my door every morning at 5:45, on the dot. We would talk and dream while we headed to our jobs. Our routine included a visit through the local drive-through to purchase a large latte and one maple bar for me. Two for him. This was Portland. Coffee is the custom. We were exhausted, caffeinated, pleased.

Ten months after we married, Jack arrived. We were thrilled. I returned to work when Jack was only a few months old. I had generous employers with a flexible, part-time schedule, nice salary, and interesting projects. My part-time consisted of three days in the office, and on my days "off," at home, I constantly checked my BlackBerry and computer, laboring over things demanding immediate attention (or so I thought). It was the nature of the corporate beast and my desire to do well. I cannot fault my employers for that. Cody spent endless hours growing his business. He paid an exorbitant rent on a commercial building because it was in the city. Usually one day a week Cody stayed home with Jack, truly a hands-on-father. Two to three times a week, I dropped Jack off with Cody's parents, the commute taking over an hour. On our days off, we tackled finishing the remodel of our house.

Cody remodeling the kitchen in our "deal" of a house

What we once perceived as the perfect urban lifestyle, we saw quite differently after Jack arrived. Our home felt cold and empty when we returned after a long day working. Our mediocre neighborhood no longer oozed with potential, more akin to a run-down, shady location with suspicious transactions happening on the corner. We questioned our decision to buy this "deal" of a house. Admittedly, in addition, I experienced the working moms' guilt for leaving my beautiful newborn. Urban, two-career family life proved not quite as idyllic as we had envisioned.

Cody vs. God

During the time we were getting to know one another, we were also getting to know God. It is said that God meets you where you are, so God met us at the bar. Actually, God met Cody on the way to the bar. Before we began dating, someone dropped off a pamphlet for a series to be held at a local church. Cody saw the pamphlet, scoffed, and tossed it in the trash can. Exactly one year later, we were dating. I was out of town, and someone dropped off a pamphlet for a series to be held at the same church. Again, Cody saw the pamphlet, scoffed, and tossed it in the trash can. One day later, Cody headed to a bar to see some friends and glanced in the trash can, seeing the pamphlet. He bent, picked it up, and read that the series started in ten minutes. He ended up on a detour to the bar that evening.

Cody chose to go to the series, in part, because of the imagery on the flyer. There was a mushroom cloud and fighter jets. It foretold the end of the world, which intrigued him. He was raised with "an angry God waiting to crush someone the moment they stepped out of line." Having left the church he grew up in, he was resigned to the fact he remained "lost and beyond redemption." He always believed in God and had faith the Bible was the true Word of God, but he did not yet know God.

A defining moment came when Cody bid on and won a job to install a culvert for a Christian family. They impressed Cody with their character, calmness, and neatness of home. He remembers them as the first people he met who genuinely seemed to know God, and love God. They were in their late sixties, and although they had hired Cody for a job, the husband labored alongside him. He answered all of Cody's questions on the subject of God without ever preaching to him. Spending time with this man gave Cody an insight that God was different than he had imagined. Undoubtedly, the man never realized the profound impact he had on Cody's life. Sometimes the smallest word or deed plants a robust seed.

Sometimes the smallest word or deed plants a robust seed.

 After his encounter with this family, Cody always looked for an opportunity to learn about this new God. When he saw the pamphlet in the trash, he saw it as a sign from God. He freely admits if he had seen it a night or two before, he likely would not have attended the series. Originally, he thought it was only one lecture on Bible prophecy and not a religious revival or series of meetings. He kept going. Cody finally began to see God was not the type of person His enemies had made Him out to be: "angry, arbitrary, and severe." Instead, he came to know "a merciful God, one who loved and cared for me like a father."

Even though I had previously requested we attend a church together, Cody was reluctant to invite me to the series. Cody recalls me "badgering him" about where he went each evening. Somehow he thought he could keep it a secret that he attended church five nights a week, for six weeks. Frankly, he wanted no one to know where he was going, including me. In fact, he actively discouraged me from going. At the time, he believed religion was for wimps and he did not want to be perceived as a wimp. Finally, I persevered. The Bible lecture series added its newest attendee. Eventually, the church gained two, and then three, regular members. Cody was baptized at the end of the series.

Homesteading Beckons

At this urban church, we met lovely Christians living out their faith in a way we yearned to do. These people had developed real relationships with the Lord. They relied upon Him and saw Him as their friend. Their lives came across as so calm compared to ours, even though they faced the same daily ups and downs. Several of them suggested that living in a rural environment provided an easier way to communicate with God. They were not as distracted by the flashing lights and entertainment that beckoned in an urban setting. They found God more readily in the quiet that nature provided, not to forsake those in the city, but to build a stronger faith, so they could aid others more effectively.

This concept along with our changed attitude toward raising Jack in the city, created an impetus for us to move to a less urban setting. Cody's parents provided day care for Jack and I did not intend to quit my job, so we began to consider finding a home and shop close to them. When we were dating, Cody took me for long, meandering drives in the area in which he grew up. One road he loved in particular. A tranquil yet expansive river flowed on one side and a wooded hillside stood on the other. Farms dotted the road and most of the homes were rather grand. Although only minutes to shopping and the freeway, at that time we thought of it as "the country."

One day we pulled into an empty lot for sale and contemplated whether it might be the lot for us. We sat in the grass under a row of apple trees and looked out over the neighboring fields. I went and knocked on the door of a neighbor's house, in the hopes someone might know something regarding the land. The gentleman knew little about the parcel and claimed nothing in the area was for sale. However, he chatted on and a lengthy conversation ensued. Later, he gave Cody and me a tour of his ragged and poorly maintained ranch home and two ramshackle sheds. A rough among diamonds. As Cody puts it, "Not a place I would have taken my shoes off inside." The house craved more than a paint job; it craved an every inch remodel. The outbuildings were too valuable to tear down, but just barely. Nonetheless, it lay only 10 minutes from Cody's parents and 25 from my job. It included a building from which Cody could work. And an acre and a half to boot. We made an offer on the property, Riverview, that very day.

Cody's dream barn at Riverview

We listed our city home while we finished negotiations with the homeowner. His children did not want him to sell Riverview, but did not aspire to buy it either. They stopped talking to him when he agreed to sell it to us. However, he refused to sign any paperwork and verbal contracts for property sales are not binding here. Finally, his son made him an offer to purchase the house and he withdrew his acceptance of our offer. Cody's dad advised us not to take it personally; it was a business transaction, and to remember: "money talks." If we wanted Riverview, offer him more.

We drove out to the country and sat in our car staring at the property we had already filled with our dreams. We talked. We prayed. We called him from the car and offered him $30,000 more than his son had. This met our top possible bid. He accepted and further confided he had not genuinely thought his son would go through with the purchase in any event.

The owner challenged our patience mightily, as he sent absurd demands to the title agency and attempted to rescind or change matters he had already accepted in writing. Eventually, we received the keys, entered, and found items missing which had been included in the purchase. When he avoided responding to our inquiries about the furniture, machinery, and tools, we let it be. We realized that for him Riverview symbolized significant events in his life and not merely real estate. He raised children, divorced, and saw happiness and sadness in that house. We recalled our city home with fondness but had not experienced the same depth of love, regret, and relief we saw in him when he sold Riverview.

I earned a comfortable salary so Cody placed his business on hold and completely remodeled the house. We added nearly 4,000 square feet onto one of the outbuildings, so Cody could run his business from home, no longer necessitating renting a separate building. Cody's dad assisted with much of the construction of the shop and house. Jack spent countless days with his doting grandmother. We relied heavily upon Cody's parents and continue to be thankful for the help they gave.

Jack with Cody's parents

Shortly after moving to Riverview is when we attended the off-grid open house event held by the author and his wife. Initially we thought we were living rurally. Our city friends certainly thought so. With the influence of our church family and the lifestyle we had seen, we determined our incremental step was not enough. We wanted a much more rugged, rural property to call home. With our two home purchases, shop addition, and on-the-go lifestyle, we needed to resolve one issue before we implemented such a change: our debt.

Our debt accumulation happened without much thought. We were responsible with our money, but somewhere along the line we accepted the lie that all debt was good. Student loan debt was "good debt." "Buy as much house as you can, you will never regret it." "Mortgage interest is tax deductible." Credit card debt "raises your credit scores," they said. So we acquired debt, because we were supposed to, and it was touted as beneficial for us financially. However, when we assessed what stood in the way of our moving to the country, debt stood at the forefront.

https://goo.gl/9AHfod

The Borrower Is Slave to the Lender

We only receive one radio station, a classical station with a limited selection of albums, the redundancy encouraging us to enjoy the silence of the countryside. At Riverview, we listened to the radio frequently, often hearing Dave Ramsey, on his nationally syndicated radio show, answer peoples' personal financial questions. He had a good sense of humor and harped continually on the necessity to "act your wage." A woman at our church, a Ramsey convert, would tell us about a class designed to combat debt called Financial Peace University. Since debt reduction was a goal of ours, more education seemed smart, and we signed up. In addition to enrolling in Ramsey's class, the guru himself happened to be giving a lecture in town right before the series of classes started. I dragged a reluctant and unenthusiastic Cody to the talk. We found Ramsey's wit engaging and believed his sincerity in wanting to help people. We drank the Kool-Aid, starting to scrimp and planning to conquer our debt.

Focusing Our Efforts

We hung an enormous poster outlining our financial obligations on our bedroom wall, painfully large, mind-boggling. Cody said, "Our debt was double what I guessed it would have been. It felt insurmountable. It was a crushing blow to our plans." I am a saver. Cody is a spender. There is often one of each in every couple. We would lie in bed, staring at the poster. "It was war." This poster now became where the spender spent his money. Cody bought an incredibly expensive poster when all was said and done.

The following are the steps we took to get out of debt: (1) stopped using credit cards, (2) built a $1,000 mini-emergency fund, (3) paid the minimum on all debts owing and tossed all extra money at our debt — smallest to largest — until paid off, (4) created a budget, (5) organized our money, and (6) tried to use cash only. These steps incorporate Ramsey's principles from his book *The Total Money Makeover,* along with a few of our own modifications. Following are some of our favorite tips.

Wranglerstar Budget Planning

Emergencies happen. Save $1,000 in an emergency fund to avoid going deeper into debt when the unexpected occurs. When you use your mini-emergency fund, because inevitably you will, remember to replenish it as quickly as possible. Our ancient Kenmore® washing machine died one morning with a clunk, refusing to agitate or spin. It had been purchased used, off Craigslist, years before. Cody attempted to fix the transmission linkage and changed the motor drive coupler, but all attempts at revival were futile.

At the same time, what we call "our double redundant system" failed. The system follows this protocol: both Cody and I go through the pockets of his clothing before I wash the dirty laundry. This system has saved countless items — pocketknives, earplugs, tape measures, wallets, receipts, screws, and nails. It also must help to keep the washing machine from breaking down as often as it might. Regrettably, we have not retrieved all cell phones from pockets prior to submerging. So in addition to needing to purchase a new, used washing machine, a new phone was also in order. Although saddened to deplete the emergency fund, we were glad to have it.

Wranglerstar budget planning

Write the Dreaded Budget

When we neglect to budget, we can engage in disheartening discussions over money. With a budget, we both know our financial limitations and goals. I am frugal and money-saving, generous but different from Cody, who would take off his coat and give it to any stranger he meets. He loves to treat others to meals and likes to buy extravagantly for others and himself. Despite occasional, severe, spending restrictions, he remains optimistic when it comes to purchasing what he wants, where I am the tragic messenger of realistic economic boundaries. I fear I break his heart a bit when I deliver messages of "wait until next paycheck" or "if we go out to eat, then we cannot buy groceries next week." We are in no sense deprived, but necessities and luxuries are not necessarily the same thing.

Eliminating debt brings great reward.

The budget is key, helping to take the emotion out of discussions concerning our financial realities. Furthermore, budgeting helps us prepare for the future. If we know money will fund a trip or a remodel, then we more easily skip eating out at a restaurant because we share a common goal, like moving to the country. When we had our debt poster, we allocated as much of our monthly finances toward debt elimination as possible. We economized, saved, and were able to knock out that debt. We were exuberant! We highly recommend doing it for anyone and everyone.

The fact of the matter remains, you must spend less than you take home. Math is math, even when it comes to budgeting. A budget shows you where you actually spend money, allows you to set aside money for non-necessities, and inspires financial creativity. In the past, I felt guilty about going to the movies or out to eat. Now, with money set aside for entertainment, I enjoy activities much more. I know our 90 minutes of fun will not put us into

Having a budget helps us to save for trips to see family, including cousins.

debt. Moreover, I no longer feel obligated to justify how we spend our money, as we have already approved and accounted for entertainment when we wrote our budget.

When we neglect to create a budget, we spend over a thousand dollars per month on groceries alone. When we write a budget, we easily cut that amount in half by eating more food from the freezer and pantry. Suddenly, we come up with additional money to allocate to other areas as well. Although a cash flow plan prepares for future spending, it also forces examination of past spending to accurately estimate how much utilities, groceries, and other items cost each month. Cody admits, "I had not been paying attention to bills and such. I didn't know where we were. It seemed like our money was evaporating." We overlooked how much we spent on certain bills until we began some serious personal accounting.

When you plan, you start to look for ways to save. Cody loves to eat out and I love going on a date. In order to stay within our cash flow plan, I now keep a list of local happy hours and two-for-one deals at our favorite restaurants. We still dine out but we might eat at 5:30 instead of 6:30, and we save substantial money.

Cut the Cards

Cut up your credit cards and use cash. Credit puts you (and us) into trouble, and it will not get you out. We were shocked to see where we owed money, realizing we were paying interest on mundane and ridiculous things. We possessed multiple student loans, several credit card bills, and a loan from a family member. We owed money for things we purchased a decade earlier. That $700 bike ended up costing $900.

Ax the credit cards

The $500 Christmas was, in reality, $650. The deals were no longer deals because we ended up paying so much for them. It stung.

Consider using cold, hard cash. We read that a study done at McDonald®'s reports consumers spend 47 percent more if using a credit or debit card than cash. You may save money merely by changing your method of payment. For me, the difficulty with which I break a $50 bill, as opposed to the ease of swiping a debit card and entering a pin number, attests to the truth of that study. Another benefit is that many businesses offer a discount for using cash. Most businesses pay three percent for the privilege of using a credit card machine, so you can often negotiate at least two percent off for paying cash. For example, our last two dentists give a discounted rate for cash up front. For them, they no longer have to wait to receive payment or spend time and money to create and send invoices for their dental services. I wish we adhered to the cash-only policy, but with our bank 40 minutes away, convenience dictates, and we often use our debit card.

When we moved into our current house, we lacked the money to purchase a refrigerator, a dishwasher, and carpet. Necessity is the mother of invention. Because it was winter, we put off buying a refrigerator for roughly three months, simply setting our food outside in the snow or in one of our unheated rooms, depending on the weather. Eventually, we accumulated enough cash to buy a used refrigerator off Craigslist. A couple gave us their broken-down dishwasher, which required no repair, only an extremely detailed cleaning. We saved for carpet for months. The old carpet joined the trash heap on the day we moved in. We painted the particleboard white until we were able to purchase matching remnants we pieced together for the bedrooms. We would love to install hardwoods but have not started saving for that yet. While the carpet falls short of our desires, it fulfills our needs and is clean, neutral, and most importantly, paid for!

It feels fantastic to have paid off all of our non-mortgage debt and to know where our money goes each month. Cody believes, "Without getting involved with Dave Ramsey, we could not have gotten out from that debt in as short an amount of time. God had a hand in that. Eliminating debt was essential for us. We were not alone in it. There was accountability. It was glorious to be able to pay it off."

Unfortunately, we must admit it worked equally well two times. Apparently, if you do not change your habits, you might fall back into debt again. Ouch! Whatever program you pick, start now!

Community

Even though living on a homestead means we have fewer literal neighbors, we still have plenty of opportunities to love our neighbors as the Bible says, and we see this exemplified by those around us as well.

Mrs. Wranglerstar and I were sitting out on the porch, and we watched our neighbor drive by with a load of firewood to deliver to another neighbor in need, and I pointed to him and said to my wife, "There goes the gospel." Our neighbor wouldn't consider himself to be a religious person. Our neighbor doesn't go to church. Our neighbor wouldn't adhere to any particular creed or dogma, but he's very close to Christ, whether he knows it or not.

The entire 66 books of the Bible can be summed up in these two things: love God and love your neighbor as yourself. What does it mean to love your neighbor as yourself? Can you really love a neighbor who treats you badly? We've had neighbors like that, so what are we to take from the teachings of the Bible that we're supposed to love someone like that? Can you make yourself love someone like that?

Do you know what it means to love your neighbor as yourself? It doesn't mean to manufacture, put on a fake pretense, or profess a love that you don't feel in your heart. Do you love yourself? When I compare myself to Christ and His character, do I love the man that I am? When I compare myself to Christ and His character, I don't love the man I am. I loathe and distrust and despise the man I am because I see the large gulf, the discrepancy between my character. So what does it mean to love your neighbor as yourself?

Do you know how we love ourselves? We love ourselves by taking care of ourselves. Do we feed ourselves three or four times a day? Do we put ourselves in good quality, comfortable clothing? Do we buy ourselves nice, warm down comforters to sleep under and wear comfortable socks and comfortable shoes? Do we give ourselves the things that give us pleasure and ease and enjoyment? Do we keep our houses warm and heated?

We love ourselves because we look after ourselves and care for ourselves. So trying to manufacture some love for

Wranglerstar:

"I was the proudest Papa in the world the day Jack cut kindling all morning to give to our neighbor and his wife. They heat with wood and he was very sick."

King Solomon:

A wise son makes a father glad, but a foolish son is a sorrow to his mother.

our neighbor that we don't have and giving lip service to that is a load of nonsense. What loving your neighbor means is providing for your neighbor the way that you would provide for yourself.

So what we're learning from this, what Christ is trying to teach us, is not to make up and give lip service to something we don't really feel; it's to provide them the things that they need. It's to give them the things that they're lacking, just like we would for ourselves. Do we see a neighbor in need who doesn't have a job? If we didn't have a job, what would we do? We would work and get ourselves a job. We would take the steps necessary to get that. Do we do the same thing for our neighbor? Do we go out and cut firewood, knowing that it's going to be cold in the winter, knowing that we need to provide for ourselves? Do we do the same thing for our neighbor? This is loving your neighbor.

The revelation took a tremendous load off of me when I finally realized that I don't have to manufacture or make something up or pretend or tell people that I feel a way that I don't. But what I can do is show real love for my neighbor by looking after them and taking care of them.

To love thy neighbor is to do and provide all these things, even to the one who despises you or treats you unkindly.

3. The Middle of Nowhere

Although we wanted to move to the countryside immediately, we figured prior to acquiring a new property we needed to finish paying off our formidable debt. We resolved to put my salary toward the debt and live off Cody's paycheck. Problematic was that we decided I should quit working before we finished eliminating our debt. We genuinely thought the Lord was telling us the time had come for me to stay at home. Family and friends freely recommended I not give up what was considered a dream job by many. This, along with the many economic justifications we found for me to keep my job, made quitting a very difficult decision. Cody admits, "It was a real challenge to give up steady, reliable income." The reality was that Cody's business did not generate quite enough to cover the bills. It presented a dilemma failing to resolve itself when crunching numbers. Despite what common sense may have dictated, we stepped out in faith.

Journey towards a new future

Honestly, it would have been difficult for me to procure an equally, well-paying job with such flexibility elsewhere, but worst-case scenario, we figured I could get some type of job. Necessity has never demanded it though. Once I quit, Cody's business skyrocketed. It was astounding. We sensed the Lord wanted to show us we could rely upon Him. He provided all we required financially. Admittedly, with our fluctuating income, we endured times with as little as one or two dollars in the bank at the end of the month. We went into debt one more time, but believe my staying home is one of the best things we have done for our family.

The Compromising Begins

As we worked on that debt, we began the task of deciding where we wanted to live. I scoured the Internet for leads on rural properties fitting our criteria. Together we climbed in our van, driving hundreds and hundreds of miles, looking at properties and towns, and crossing specific areas off the maps as "not for us" locations.

Men and women can think very differently on the topic of moving to the country. The reality and the fantasy are not the same. Men imagine moving to a rural property as "The Great Adventure" — wood to cut, buildings to construct, fields to plant, risks to be taken, and great stories to tell. Women picture "Isolated Domestic Drudgery" — stuck in a sod hut lacking modern conveniences, canning and sewing with no friends around, tending the children, and whacking a broom at country mice. In most cases, they are both correct. To a certain degree, realities can vary from a large yard with an oversized garage smack in town, to an off-grid, no appliance home, with mountains and trees as your only friends.

Cody claimed he would choose the latter — happy to move to extremely rural Montana or Idaho, emerging for human contact on an annual basis. I adamantly opposed the suggestion. I aimed to see people at least bi-annually! Truthfully, although an introvert, I like to see people frequently. As a family, we love to be with people but desperately crave alone time, too. Jack and Cody complain if we schedule too many activities per week. I like to see friends or neighbors every week or so. Because of my "need" for relationships, we set our location search to be within 60 minutes of a small town and within five hours of Portland. This would allow us to drive back to see relatives and friends on most holidays and be fairly close to an airport and bigger shopping selections. Moreover, it would be convenient enough to a small town to be part of a community, become involved, and fulfill basic shopping necessities.

In addition, we desperately wanted an important, quirky location requirement — sunshine. The house at Riverview had an enormous shortcoming — a three-season stream ended in a magnificent, 20-foot waterfall, visible from the kitchen and living room windows. The picturesque waterfall cascaded down a rock ravine with gigantic emerald and ruddy-hued cedars on either side. Stunning. Unfortunately, the hillside down which the waterfall fell from blocked the sun for months each year. We suspected we were turning into ferns. Wonderful, but causing deficiencies in necessary vitamin D.

"I Will Never"

We quickly narrowed down the areas in which we wished to live. Providentially, Cody and I were both attracted to the same type of climate. The mountains of the Pacific Northwest (PNW)can create

My parents also helped us search.

diverse microclimates in a relatively small area. Temperatures, terrain, view — all shift wildly as you draw near the coast or a mountain range, a river, gorge, or plateau. Much to most peoples' surprise, the PNW is not merely a soggy green paradise. There are barren deserts, open skies, and sun galore. Our narrowing simply meant we were still in a vast area of consideration, but finally able to use online search engines to aid us. We focused on a 3,500 square mile region with several exclusions within that area.

Both sets of parents drove around with us while we evaluated communities and potential home sites. In four short years of marriage, Cody and I had already been through two major home remodels and a huge addition to a shop. The skills we had honed were both a blessing and a curse, as we thought we could "fix" most anything, allowing us to consider every possible property for sale. Over the course of a year, we looked at many properties in the area we had defined, but found three true contenders.

Our first real "find" was a delightful, picturesque Swedish cope log cabin — newly built with a large insulated shop on 20 acres with a pond and mountain view. It was close to a little town, but not too close. The owners gave us a tour, telling us where they hoped to relocate in order to be closer to their daughter and grandchildren. The husband clearly did not wish to move and lamented he hoped to find a small acreage with a shop close to the city. Unbeknownst to them, our home fit their "want" list to a tee — minutes from their family, two shops, a garage, and a lovely renovated home (if I may say so myself). At this time, we had not yet put Riverview on the market or even prepared it for showing.

After that day of touring, we drove home, crunched numbers, began preparing the house to show the cope log cabin owners, and started email discussions for a house "swap." They came to visit our home and outbuildings and the negotiations proceeded with intensified vigor. They asked if they could begin to move their belongings to one of our shops. It looked as if we had found our home in the country. Both sides believed their homes to be worth at least $100,000 over the others'. Ultimately, our differences could not be resolved. Their home still sits for sale, empty. Seven years later, it is listed at the price we initially offered them (in full disclosure, Riverview ultimately sold for what they offered us). It sits a few miles from where we now live.

Another property we visited repeatedly was reached by walking over an easement on private land and then through state land, and over a footbridge to a scenic wood lot. However, this was not the legal access — it was 20 minutes away, washed out years earlier, no one knew exactly where it should be located, and the property owners did not want it put back in. The legal easement would be expensive to install and maintain because of the exceeding steepness of the property. Problematic with purchasing undeveloped land in the foothills of a mountain is the confluence of steep slopes, creeks and rivers, forests, and lack of access. Yes, bridges and roads can be put in (after the environmental paperwork and permitting), but often there is a reason no one has developed some of these parcels. Given Cody's background in excavating, we were not

Even Jack helped us look for property.

Some property was difficult to reach.

Searching for property

afraid of putting roads in what appeared to be near-impossible locations, but sometimes we could not justify the financial risk. We had succeeded in eliminating our debt and sought to be smart with the equity we planned to receive from the sale of Riverview. The cost of the inaccessible property, plus its development was more than we were willing to invest. After years and years on the market, the price plummeted, and someone recently purchased it. We pass the driveway on our way home from town.

The only other property we seriously considered was a newly built ranch with large barn, 20 acres, and stunning mountain view. While we drove to it, I remember saying I would never live this far out. Fortunately, Cody and his parents concurred the drive was too long from town. It was a rainy, cold day, and nothing about the place sold itself. Today, we know the view is spectacular, the house is well-planned and inviting, and the drive is the perfect distance from town. Our next-door neighbors live there.

I mention that these properties lie close to where we live now for a reason. While we searched for property, we prayed to the Lord to open and close doors to reveal where He wanted us to go. We believed this region was where we were supposed to relocate. Despite this feeling, one day, feeling a bit dejected we were not finding an acceptable home, I adjusted the location parameters of my ritual, online search for properties. A few new interesting properties popped up, so we set up appointments to go and view them.

Mrs. Wranglerstar and Jack

Sign on the Dotted Line

We preferred to head out on our own when viewing prospects, but met with an agent for one potential property, a serious contender. We then headed off to meet with the owner of the off-grid development called Noble Valley. Paul Larson picked us up and drove up a ragged and pothole-filled gravel road. The drive wandered between enormous trees, a rushing river raged below, and in the distance, a mountain popped into view. A bobcat crossed in front of us. It was as though Mr. Larson had planned it all. We walked through a locked gate and up a steep curving hill, bringing expectations around the bend. Magnificent. We swooned as we drove up the long straight driveway, connecting the numerous 20-plus acre plots. Each off-grid. Each facing the valley and the mountain across the way.

We clambered out of the pickup to face the beaming Mr. Larson, his face aglow with the excitement of someone wanting to share something spectacular. We walked and walked, uphill and down on an old logging road connecting the distant lots. Only one other family resided with the Larsons in the development, and they had chosen the first lot. As we approached the end of the road, we could see on the map there remained one lot we had not yet explored. Paul explained, "It is a special lot. We are not interested in selling it." Despite his admonition, we walked it. We returned with him to his house, met his lovely wife, and spent hours talking in their cozy mountain home.

Cody and I returned home elated with the multiple possibilities the day had presented. We liked the first lot we saw with the agent, but we loved the various lots at the off-grid development. One talent we both possess is the ability to imagine buildings constructed where they do not exist, walls torn down and new ones built — a sort of construction visualization gift. To us, Noble Valley's steep, timbered, rocky terrain could be tamed. We prayed. We talked. We slept on it. Two days later, we brought Cody's parents up to see the properties. The Larsons homesteaded this remote location about 15 years earlier, building much themselves, and raising and homeschooling their four kind, God-loving, successful children. We determined to raise Jack there too. If everything proceeded as planned, they would be our nearest neighbors, roughly three-quarters of a mile up a mountain road (not yet put in).

Even though we believed we were supposed to live in the area where the first three properties were, and where we now reside, we ignored that impression. We knew, we undoubtedly knew, we wanted the lot not for sale. There was a bit of forbidden fruit about it. Splendid, with chante-relles hiding under massive trees, moss, and ferns, and dropping steeply into a raging river the neighbors had never even attempted to reach. The mountain was regularly encased in fog gracing itself above the valley. The other lots were similarly glorious. This one simply beckoned a bit more. Is that not the way it always works? It violated our budget and location criteria. Despite this, we desired to purchase it anyway.

The Larsons knew we wanted the lot that was not for sale, but had not initially desired to sell it. They threw out a figure higher than we planned to pay for raw land. Not an unfair figure, simply more than we budgeted. We should have stopped and deliberated more before purchasing the lot. We did not. Instead, we proceeded to make a thousand mistakes. First, our offer to purchase the Noble Valley property was above what we planned to spend for raw land. Moreover, the projected costs associated with developing a remote, off-grid parcel, were more than we planned. Financially, we had enough to build, but it stretched our budget to the max. Second, we made the offer while Riverview had not yet sold. We had not even listed it yet. Dumb. Third, we ignored the valuable wisdom of those who loved us. Although our families and friends thought we were a little crazy for wanting to leave our beautiful shop and home near the city, they were all encouraging. However, with this little endeavor, their concern grew immensely; heads shook, murmuring occurred, and questions abounded about what were we thinking. We were living our fantasy, instead of the reality of life. Fourth, and most gravely, we thanked the Lord for His assistance up to this point and decided we could take it from there. I suspect once we chose to follow our own path — even ignoring common sense — then the Lord left us up to our own devices.

I believe the Lord leads us if we ask Him. If we listen, the Holy Spirit suggests what we should do. He is our conscience — the little voice telling us right from wrong, to check up on someone, to stop, to be still. He suggests, but we are always allowed to make our own decisions. The Lord has given us free will. Use it. Do what you like, but realize there are always consequences for action — both good and bad consequences impacting us, and others who are not always engaged in the decision-making process. Unfortunately, this started a difficult period for us individually and as a couple. Our actions affected many others.

After entering into a contract to purchase the Noble Valley parcel, we made our down payment, and began making monthly payments. Tight but doable. Moving toward our dream of living off-grid as a stay-at-home family, we found ourselves in a position with no debt, except the mortgage, and with Cody's business booming. We purchased the Noble Valley property and were of the opinion we were finally on our way. All we had left to do was construct a new home and sell Riverview. Regrettably, the recession hit. We were stuck with two mortgages. We had been putting the final touches on Riverview to put it on the market and it became incumbent for us to do so immediately. We received glowing reports from the real estate broker who seemed so confident our house would sell quickly. It did not. While we were never late with either mortgage, we were scraping by. The financial stress and workload at our two properties wore upon us.

Thank You God, We Will Take it From Here

The housing market recession was in full swing. Eventually, we called in new realtors to see if they might want to take over the sale of our home. While they liked our home, they suggested some expensive landscaping to curb some of the noise from the traffic on the country road on which we lived. We felt awful. We did not possess the money for the landscaping, even doing the job ourselves. As we thought over if we should switch realtors, we ached with the stress of it all. What had we gotten ourselves into?

Sunset in Noble Valley

Finally, the same week, two years after we bought the Noble Valley property and 18 months after beginning the house-selling ordeal, we received an offer contingent upon the sale of the buyers' home. We did our research and found their home nice, but overpriced. Signing the contingency agreement would force us to take our house off the market while we waited for theirs to sell. Before the deadline to sign on the dotted line, we received another offer. Lower in price but a cash offer.

Two offers in one week after such an extended time. They were not what we hoped for, but beggars cannot be choosers, and we were on our knees. The cash offer released us from countless mortgage appraisal requirements difficult to acquire when it comes to unique rural properties, which we had.

Their inspector was ridiculously thorough. We surmised he had been the victim of a house fire, been sued for a bad inspection, or recently been through fire inspection training. Even though professionals rebuilt the fireplace less than five years earlier, he insisted we get it re-tucked, cleaned, re-inspected, and more. The oil tank required decommissioning. The septic tank needed maintenance. The purchasers were incredibly reasonable and easy to work with. Fortunately, they allowed us to stay in our home for a few months after closing. This gave us cash in hand without forcing us to move out immediately to the undeveloped, off-grid Noble Valley property.

Gaining a Foothold

Using the sales price of the house and the income Cody was still bringing in, we rewrote our financial plan to reflect what we actually had to spend, instead of what we had hoped. Disappointed but still financially able, we finished preparing the land so we would be able to build the shell of our home and hunker down for the winter. We had spent the previous year and a half clearing timber and pushing in a rough road. Prior to the rough road, Cody needed to winch his truck from tree to tree merely to reach the property line. This was rugged country. Cody logged the road and house site single-handedly. However, when the downed logs were ready for skidding to the landing, I looked tough enough to be a choker setter (someone who attaches cables around logs, then moves clear, so the equipment operator can pull the logs). Apparently, I appeared to be a limber, too (someone who saws the branches and limbs off a piece of fallen timber). Then he strapped chainsaw chaps on me, outfitted me with a helmet and googles, put a Stihl Ms260 in my clutches, and set me to work. I only dropped an enormous log on my foot once before learning to be more careful about foot placement. It still hurts occasionally. Good hard work.

Mrs. Wranglerstar
working the chain saw

During our planning process we wanted to build both a large shop and modest house. In their numerous years of living there, the Larsons had not built a shop, not even a garage or carport. Substantial snow fell and each trip down the mountain included shoveling out a vehicle. As needed, they had repaired the tractor and snowplow on a gravel pad in whatever the weather dealt. There was no decent place to store tools and implements. The yet pushed-in road to our property would be steep and winding. In talking over the issue with Mr. Larson, we contemplated putting a larger, joint shop on his property. We even hired a lawyer to write up an agreement regarding ownership, construction, and use of the building. However, with our construction budget rewritten, we scrapped the plan. Even a second building for a shop was not attainable in the near future. Cody's dad drew up plans for a large shop with the house on top. This way we only paid for one roof, one foundation, and one set of walls, thus decreasing our costs substantially. Because of the steep terrain, it would appear to be a ranch house but include full access to the shop from below. We brought the plans to an engineer who began work on the septic system and house/shop.

An Exceedingly Rough Road

Up and down the mountain road to Noble Valley we drove. Think third-world road. The steep winding road calls for caution. It is a harrowing road where anything can happen. Throw in 45 minutes of potholes and rocks to town in fair weather. Another 10 to the storage units to rummage for indispensable tools. Another 20 beyond for a sizeable

Cody working at Noble Valley. He put in the road on which he is standing.

The big yellow "lemon"

hardware store. One day Cody suffered two flat tires, rolling up to the Larsons' on a flattened spare. He borrowed a truck and headed back down the road to fix the flats. Back up to return the truck. Tires changed. Then began the hour and a half drive home. Money and time spent. Nothing on the project done.

Shortly before we purchased Noble Valley, Cody started our YouTube channel. In part, we used it to show the development of the land and house site to our family who lived far away. YouTube was in its infancy, and people did not consider the privacy of the videos the way they do now. So while we were able to show my parents the development adventures we participated in, other people began to watch. Some were friends and others strangers. While I disliked showing our life online, Cody appreciated the advice he received.

We had been the unfortunate purchasers of an immense hunk of metal that generally failed to run. The bulldozer, a 1969 International Dresser TD20B, ran well when we purchased it. Afterward, it only ran occasionally, with a preference for reverse. The machine was so big it took over a hundred gallons to change the fluids. With YouTube and the help of an elderly mechanic, Cody rebuilt the transmission on it, not once, but twice. A greasier, more disheartened man you have never met. He learned what it was like to work in Mr. Larson's "shop," even in the pouring rain and on freezing, windy days. Thousands of dollars, countless hours, the help of friends, and that piece of steel still refused to run. The bulldozer finally elected to quit altogether. We sold it for scrap.

We devised a way to transport it down the driveway and off the mountain to a meeting spot along the road. The morning of pick up, wouldn't you know it, the bulldozer started like a dream and ran perfectly. Cody was thrilled to be able to drive it to the meeting spot. The driver who was picking up the dozer took the corner of the road too closely and his lowboy fell over the edge. As it was the only road in and out for miles, traffic began to back up on this otherwise nearly empty road. The way was narrow, so cars could not pass. No cell coverage out there. We were not getting off to a good start with our future neighbors.

Cody was supposed to meet the lowboy miles up the road for pick up, but instead had to drive over an hour, and yes, drive it in reverse. Eventually, we used the dozer to pull out the truck. The driver was not happy and a bit embarrassed (particularly because we had warned him about the corner, knowing its history). It is a deceptive corner, even with highly cautious drivers. At last count, we heard dozens (yes, plural) of vehicles have slipped over the edge. I admit it was brilliant to see that dozer trucked off.

Nevertheless, we had a ton of work to finish (literally!). Machinery was essential to push a better road to the property, prep the site, dig the foundation, and handle all of the timber. Because Cody previously operated heavy equipment, he could complete the jobs. After pricing rentals, we ending up buying a used excavator we hoped to keep for future use on the rugged terrain we would call home. After our bulldozer experience, we chose to buy a newer model excavator we knew would run.

For delivery of the excavator, we hired the man who delivered the bulldozer, as he had previously driven the road without incident. Nonetheless, we again cautioned him regarding the corner. Despite the warning, we saw his wheel go over the corner's edge with our beautiful excavator. Hanging. Dangling. Again, it stopped traffic both ways for hours, the trucker pale in the face. Everyone's full attention was focused on coming up with a solution. Because of the truck's position, we could not drive the excavator off the truck bed. Its weight caused a creaking and groaning. Fortunately, a neighbor was logging in the area with his Caterpillar bulldozer. He set some chains here and there and used the Cat to pull with all its might. The truck bed slowly eased up on the road. The trucker kept going without mishap and likely swore never to return there.

Steep, rough roads made for dangerous driving conditions.

Our road in Noble Valley as it washed away

As we started putting the rough driveway in, Cody's parents generously provided a large fifth wheel for us to stay in while we were on the mountain. It felt luxurious to take a shower, turn on the stove, and stock a functioning refrigerator. Formerly, we drove both ways or slept in our van and prayed for no rain. To us, the fifth wheel was a mansion. We also made use of a small 24-foot fifth wheel belonging to Cody's granddad, and turned it into a tool shed. The trailer leaked like a sieve so we tarped the top to protect our tools and supplies from the damp. In addition to a tool shed, the little trailer became a home for our two barn cats that moved with us into the wilderness.

The Coming Storm

Eventually, my mom flew in and helped us pack up our house and shops. We loaded box after box into an old U-Haul® van borrowed from a friend. We then filled seven storage units with household items, tools, and equipment. Additionally, we left pallet racking, scaffolding, and our flatbed trailer outside of our former neighbor's shop. With the house sold and emptied, the excavator delivered, and a rough road put in, we launched into further preparing the house site, installing the septic system and finishing the water well. We measured and leveled, excavated, and smoothed by hand. Cody put in tremendous hours on the excavator, often barely able to stand up straight when staggering off, because of the jarring of his body for such an extended period, days on end. He admitted the stress of the steep terrain and sheer cliffs caused his body to tense, which exacerbated the soreness he was experiencing. For the first time in his life, he wore the seat belt because of the danger involved.

I became an expert at using the ground level, but only after Cody explained multiple times. He repeatedly spoke the foreign language of construction to which I was not privy. He practiced his patience with the unlearned. Overall, I became fairly adept in chainsaw use, setting chokers, estimating slopes, watching myself around heavy equipment, efficiently digging holes, the proper use of a rake, and on and on. Jack easily won the dirty child award, but we heard no complaints from him concerning his hours of playing outside.

The race to finish was on. As our neighbor put it, "We had less than ten weeks until the snow hit." Some fifth wheels are insulated and made for winter snows, but not ours. On the mountain the previous winter, the weather strained the vehicle to its limits. When the snow dumped, we drove over two hours each way in order to shovel snow off the roof. The roof was so thin we feared the shovel would pierce it. We attempted to use the leaf blower to relieve the roof of the snow. All that did was soak us. While we made a valiant attempt to keep the roof snow-free, leaks began. While we were gone, water soaked the carpets, causing mold. Towels were dripping upon our arrival. The humidity caused the cabinet doors to swell to the point where they would no longer open or shut. Additionally, the mice moved in, poking out their country heads when we would open drawers and scratching the walls all night long.

We knew in the winter the trip from town took even longer than usual, lengthening substantially depending upon the amount of snow on the ground. The road was one of the last the county plowed, and days could go by before it was clear. When there was snow, we would drive up and in as far as we could on an old logging road and then snowshoe to our property. We lugged gas for the generator, food, clothes, and towels for leaks, etc. in army surplus Alice backpacks. Sometimes we carried a sleeping or exhausted little boy through the snow, too. On more than one occasion, the Larsons loaned us their snowmobile, alleviating the need to carry the heavy fuel and propane we burned through so quickly.

Pretty but impassable — the logging road in winter

For the health of the fifth wheel, and the ability to keep it warmer, thus necessitating less lugging of fuel, we hoped to pull our home on wheels inside before it began snowing. We wanted to frame and rough in the shell of the house, among other jobs, in the next ten weeks. In an effort not to drain our financial resources completely, Cody continued to work from the shop while we still lived at Riverview and then out of the storage garages. It was less than ideal.

Perhaps it was merely because we were doing things ourselves or building an off-grid relatively inexpensive home, but we sensed resistance from

the various governmental agencies at every turn. The officials lacked the "let's get the job done" attitude we desperately desired and needed. We had submitted a myriad of paperwork, pulled all the permits, dotted our i's and crossed our t's, and yet the departments did not seem to know what to do with us. We were trying to hit a moving target with continuous requests for changes in engineering and permitting requirements. Additionally, because of the steep terrain, we were required to hire an engineering firm for a geotechnical report and have the structural engineer make numerous adjustments in our building plans. We wondered if the county officials were reluctant to give permit approval over fear they might become liable for unforeseen problems in the future. Even with these additional costs, we were still within budget, and on schedule, to be in a covered structure before fall rains and winter snow hit.

https://goo.gl/LAe6Gm

Wisdom from the Journey

Buyer Beware

Once you decide to take the plunge and move to the countryside, remember there is no perfect property. Your requirements change according to what you hope to accomplish on your land and what property is available. Listed below are things to mull over and how to find and finance that special property.

Access is Important

Road — Is there well-maintained road frontage? Do you want a paved road reliably plowed in winter or is a gravel road acceptable? Does the county plow and grate the road? Here, roads are plowed quickly, but at least within two days. However, our county does nothing to alleviate dust associated with gravel roads. Gravel roads face potholes, mud, and washboarding. Part of the year, you may be able to drive 50 miles per hour on it and 25 the rest — your half-hour commute becomes an hour. How would you cope with such an erratic schedule when planning for work and school? Years ago, the county wanted to pave two of the roads in our area. The community fought it because they wanted to ensure there was not an increase in traffic, as pavement provides a scenic route for bicyclists and motorcyclists who avoid the gravel now. Less pavement equals less traffic, but longer drive times.

At one of our rural locations, over 20 culverts along the road required inspection regularly to ensure proper drainage or replacement if they failed. This was a steep road which frequently washed out during heavy rains. This would be a terrifically expensive road to maintain if it were private. Although this is a county road, upkeep remains scant, potholes plentiful, and complaints to the county common. Required maintenance and actual maintenance can be different things. By law, how regularly does your road have to be paved, plowed, swept, and graveled? One

county road, which leads to good friends, is inaccessible for a good portion of the year. The long route adds an extra 35 minutes.

Driveway — If the driveway is exceedingly long, how will you pay for gravel? Or plow it in the winter? A shovel might not cut it. While you can pay someone else, barter, or trade jobs, it costs you either time or money. Is your property part of a road association where you pay for maintenance? Even if you own equipment that could do the job? What is the annual fee? Also, consider seasonal flooding and dust issues. In late summer, I dissuade Jack from riding his quad on our driveway because it creates so much dust.

Does your property location necessitate a four-wheel drive vehicle, boat, or snowmobile? Some friends can drive to their home in the summer but must snowshoe or snowmobile in the winter. Other friends hold an easement across a logging company's property, upon which their driveway runs. Their once-smooth, graveled mile and half road is now a deep-rutted, muddy mess due to the weight of the logging trucks driving on it in the rain. They complained to the logging company, but do not have a legal leg to stand on, and must pay for repairs themselves. Cody and I have spoken plenty of times about only owning one four-wheel drive vehicle, a truck to haul things, and a small two-wheel drive car getting good gas mileage for our long driving sessions to town and back. Inevitably, days after the discussion, I leave on a sunny, lovely day and the weather quickly changes, necessitating four-wheel drive on the way home. Similarly, when the schedule dictates that we head out immediately, the truck will be loaded with tools and wood and too dirty for "town clothes." Our road is well maintained, but I would be loathe to give up my four-wheel drive. For me it has become a necessity.

Access affects mail. Neighbors have a long driveway connecting to a private road. UPS and FedEx choose not to deliver to them if the road is muddy, so our front porch is now their front porch for package delivery. USPS delivers to their mailbox at the end of the road but expects them to come into town for large package pickup. Access matters.

Easements — Check for road easements associated with the property. Having them is not necessarily a deal-breaker, but you should understand the terms and location of the easements. Sometimes easements benefit you, such as accessing your property if it is landlocked. Many states do not want landlocked parcels to sit empty and wasted, so mandate access though neighboring properties as a legal right — but access can come at a steep cost. Verify that easements are in writing. If property changes hands, then lack of a written record of the terms of any oral agreement can cause confusion, allegations of trespass, and legal hassles.

Easements also exist for water, mineral, oil, timber, and railroad rights. Understand the potential ramifications of any rights associated with the property. What does reasonable access to land mean for development and production of the right? Do subsurface rights exempt them from any effects of damage to the appearance or use of land? For example, companies cash in on their mineral, oil, or fracking rights, leaving unsuspecting landowners surprised by the details of terms in purchase agreements.

Water?

Is there a reliable source of water meeting your needs? Do you only require enough water for your home and a personal garden or do you plan to farm and own livestock? Water laws vary significantly in the eastern and western portions of the United States, and state to state, so double-check that you have a legal right

to water before purchasing the property. Simply because someone is using water on their farm does not mean they hold the legal right to use it. When there is plenty of water, no one may complain about extra use, but during drought years, any excess water use can be curtailed, causing crops to die and orchards to wither. Water rights might be separate from the property upon which the water is located. This means you might not be able to use water from the pond or stream on your property. Even if you hold a water right, someone downstream or on a neighboring property may have priority to use that water. Furthermore, endangered species can claim rights to water that may originate far from where the species lives. In some locations, like Colorado, legislators banned the storage of rainwater for personal use, and even the reuse of greywater. Exemptions often exist to use water for personal use, but make certain you possess a water right or fall within the legal exemption. If you have a right, use it, or you may legally lose it!

Is there enough water for your home, animals, orchard, garden, and ponds? In many parts of the West, wells dry up. It can be quite expensive to dig deeper or dig a new well. Be positive you inquire about volume and if it is seasonal or abundant year-round. Check with your state's natural resources and/or health departments to obtain information concerning water rights and wells associated with the property and water. Is there already a well on the property? Is it deep? Is there water in it? Do you have a legal right to access water on your neighbor's property? You

want to guarantee there exists a legal right to water.

All private wells in our state are supposed to be registered. This does not mean they are. Check how far the water source is from any potential contamination sources such as manure storage, barns, or septic systems. Our well is downhill from the barn, which is generally not advisable, but it is nearly one-quarter of a mile so it passes muster. What is the quality of the water? Is the water potable? Our water tastes funny, containing copious amounts of minerals. We filter it before drinking. Get your water tested and be positive you

can treat it with something as simple as a filter. When purchasing, make sure that if you cannot find water or it is too contaminated, you can walk away from the deal.

Some friends rent property where the water line runs above ground. This functions fine in the summer, but if the temperature drops below freezing, the pipes freeze and they must truck water in for their use. Dirty laundry is hauled into town. They regularly shower at friends' and relatives' home — all six of them. Water remains one of those things to chew on (sip on?), even if you rent.

Consider the Land

You want to look at soil type, fertility, aspect (direction a slope faces), slope, drainage, and a history of what has been done on the property previously. Many counties now post maps online showing the topography and soil type of the land. In this way, you can conduct preliminary research before even visiting a site. Information regarding ravines, cliffs, hillsides, water location, power lines, and wind turbines may not be mentioned in the sales information but easily acquired online.

If the land was farmed, did they use a large number of pesticides and fertilizers? What crops were grown? What is growing there now? Livestock grazed? Is there fertility left in the soil? Can you improve the fertility? Does the current soil type support the plans you hope to achieve? You can find out from your local United States Department of Agriculture Natural Resources Conservation Service office what soil types cover your property. The maps indicate the soil productivity, which is a measure of the soil's capacity to grow plants and trees.

Does the property contain wetlands? Is it in a flood zone? Drainage issues may curtail plans to farm or build. While this might be unmanageable for some uses, you might be able to negotiate a better price because of it. Flooding in the Pacific Northwest can cause landslides. Study where you want to put that new home in relationship to a steep hillside and a raging river before you build.

What was the land used for before? Talk to the neighbors; do some research. We found out one of the properties we acquired had housed a welding shop. The previous owner was not particularly tidy, so we picked a spot for our garden farther away from that shop than we otherwise might have. We are glad we did. We found a ton of metal in the ground and cannot imagine what chemicals were spilt or poured out. If it was previously a working farm, you are apt to run into lots of broken glass, twine, and metal. We do. It is the nature of a hard-working farm, but is vastly different than if someone leaves a virtual landfill.

Are there copious amounts of weeds? Some counties mandate eradication of select weeds. Will you spray or acquire livestock who eat that type of weed? If you neglect to eliminate the weeds, the county might spray and then send you the bill.

If the land is zoned for commercial use, be positive you are not inheriting a slew of environmental issues. We know of one property where they found out their location had previously been a gas station and leaking tanks were suspected. While the previous owner was held responsible for cleanup, they sat with an enormous ugly hole in their front yard for over a year.

New, Used, or Converted?

Are there houses, outbuildings, and fences? Great, prepare to move right in. Or not. If requiring repairs, getting professionals out to distant locations can be more expensive than in town. Whenever we estimate the cost and time it should take to finish a job we multiply it by three and then get pretty accurate numbers.

One forgotten part or bolt can cost hours driving to the nearest hardware store and extra money in gas and wear and tear to the car.

Nowadays it can be cheaper to buy already developed property rather than raw land. The costs of permitting, engineering, and code compliance have risen dramatically. At one time, you only suffered through inspections for basic structural, electrical, and plumbing. Most counties require a fully constructed home instead of only a shell before releasing a permit to habitat the dwelling. Even if you wanted to use an outhouse and kerosene lamps and rough it while you build, you may be legally precluded from doing so. Weigh the benefits of building a little apartment over a shop or garage to get you on your property. This eliminates driving back and forth while completing construction of a home. Keep in mind that RVs, campers, and fifth-wheel trailers are often not allowed as primary residences on raw land, even if you plan on building later.

Consider converting a building from one use to another. One building we had was a barn but we needed a shop. We cleared the stalls and poured concrete floors and, presto, shop! Previous owners of our home wanted an exercise room, so they enclosed the carport, resulting in a cavernous, awkward, nearly windowless room (and this is why we use the term remuddle instead of remodel). While we save up for some serious

remodels, we keep telling ourselves our house has good bones. Unfortunately, many of the doors, windows, cabinets, and interior walls are in the wrong places, impeding the sunlight from pouring in and also obstructing the view.

Are there fences? Do not assume fences are situated accurately on the parcel's boundary. We know of one family who had 19 acres but zoning minimums were 20 to build. They simply fenced in an acre of their neighbor's and called it their own. They were found out. However, if someone does this long enough they can legally own the land (usually 10 to 20 years). Another story we were told involved a family who inaccurately situated their barn, with part of it on the neighboring parcel. Oops. Look for boundary pins and pay for a survey if you must build that close to a boundary line.

On or Off the Grid?

For first-world comfort, utilities are vital, including sewer, electricity, phone service, Internet, and garbage. Remember, county governments often cannot offer the same amount or level of services you find in a more urban or suburban setting.

If the property has its own systems, you want to check the condition of each. A full septic system or leaking sewer line is not particularly fun to deal with. Once we had a pipe break off on the inside of our septic tank — an especially disgusting job I was happy to hand off (sorry, Honey!).

At Noble Valley, Cody and I installed a septic system together. It is not a difficult job, but it took renting machinery, buying the system parts, carefully leveling ditches and properly installing the system. Then, there were inspections before hooking it up to the indoor plumbing. Despite Cody's experience with putting in hundreds of septic systems as

Solar panels can be an option.

an excavator, the county required us to pay one hundred dollars to take a written exam in order to procure a septic installer's certificate to work under the permit. Cody heard about the requirement and said, "I'm too busy. Besides, you are much better at taking tests." So, yes, address any of your septic system installation questions my way. I was certified.

If there is not municipal power, how expensive is it to bring to your home? Power lines cost thousands of dollars per mile for single-phase lines running overhead. If an area requires lines be buried, the price can more than double. Electric companies commonly assess additional hookup fees and basic monthly rates plus actual use charges.

A couple we know live off-grid and were quoted $60,000 to bring electrical in 20 years ago. They decided to install a solar system, which performed adequately. As town moved closer, they considered connecting and were recently quoted $6,000 to get on the grid. The wife says it would be nice to use a toaster, clothes dryer, and hair dryer. Usually small-scale solar, hydro, and wind power cannot support such energy-draining appliances. She would no longer need to plan when to run the vacuum or start the generator when the batteries run low. Her husband could finally operate regular tools in his shop. It is important to take into account the cost of the system, how it affects your daily living situation, and specialized tools and appliances you might require. If there is electricity on your property, is it in the outbuildings too? If you select solar and wind power, are you capable of maintaining it if something goes wrong? How reliable is the power? The first winter we were in our current home, we lost power for eight days… in a row. Can you afford a generator? We are saving for solar panels but feel fortunate to be tied to the grid until we get them.

How will you heat or air-condition your home? Will you heat with wood? Will heating your home burn three or 13 cords of wood? In your region, how much does an acre of forest produce of new wood each year? Use these numbers to calculate how many acres it would take to sustain your forest with continued logging for heating purposes.

With cell phones becoming ubiquitous, the landline may no longer be a necessity. Our cell phones functioned great for years until there was an immensely powerful windstorm. Suddenly we lost nearly all coverage. Then the best way to call was if I positioned myself in the north part of the house, in the upper bedroom, lying down. Not particularly fantastic for business calls. We ended up paying for a landline. Then we upgraded our cell phones and, lo and behold, we again enjoy cell coverage. Ask neighbors what cell coverage works best where you live; most have stood out in the driveway trying to get reception.

Internet can be tricky. We were excited to see fiber optic cable being laid down our road and beyond. We waited to hear when we could finally connect to high-speed Internet. Then we heard companies receive government grants to lay the cable in rural areas but have no obligation to hook the community up. I am not convinced this is true, but three years later no high-speed anything exists here. In addition, we cannot contract for Internet through our local phone service provider. That leaves satellite: a slow, expensive, and very limited option. As our only option, it remains the one we use. We frequently "run out" of Internet. We only receive a limited amount of downloads each day. This typically allows us to answer emails, view a few videos (in the low-resolution setting), and occasionally watch a movie. More often than not, we exhaust our data cap at the very best part of the movie. If a large file downloads or something updates on our computers or phones, we inadvertently deplete our entire data supply by mid-afternoon. So if we neglect to respond, it is not avoidance, it is our Internet connection.

Garbage service? Recycling service? Our closest dump and recycling center lies 50 minutes away. If you have garbage service but not recycling, will you store glass and plastic until you can make the drive? Cody's sister and her husband designated a little-used trailer as their recycling/trash hauler and head to the dump every few months. Recently, a bear confirmed, "One man's trash is another bear's treasure." After making a mess for dinner, the bear hit the chicken coop and beehives for dessert. They hope 5,000 volts will dissuade the bear if he comes back for seconds.

If garbage service is at the end of your lengthy driveway, how do you lug your dirty, stinky, leaking garbage can back and forth each week? New truck? While it may not sound like a huge inconvenience, these types of rural hassles happen each week, for years, and add up to take time from your day.

What Is the Zone?

The local government regulates all property through zoning and property taxes. It is important to know what the property is zoned for: residential use, mixed-use, commercial, industrial, agricultural, forestry, etc. What do you want to do and does it comply with zoning? Do your neighbors care about the zoning? Do they break a multitude of the regulations? What if you build a successful farm or business, despite the zoning, and later face legal action to stop your activity?

Jack with property pin.

Counties have different zoning and permitting

Property may need cleaning up

requirements. You cannot build on all raw land. Some friends inherited property upon which they could build, but years later parcel size minimums increased and their lot was no longer buildable. Because the county gave them ample notice that lot sizes were increasing, they were not grandfathered in. We looked at two properties having a special recreational zoning. As I recall, this meant you could only use it for three months of the year. Hardly the place to put down full-time roots.

Include a way to terminate contracts if you find you cannot build or the buildings were not properly permitted when built. If necessary, obtain legal documents showing the county or town will issue building permits on unpermitted buildings or the raw land before you buy.

Additionally, ensure you buy or build a suitable house for the neighbor-hood. One family built a multi-million dollar mansion in the middle of small farms and properties with modest homes. When they put in on the market, no one bought it because it was so out of place. Then they attempted to rent it out as a destination for large parties and weddings. While people came, the neighbors quickly grew annoyed with late night parties. They contacted the owners who refused to close their rental operation. The owners ultimately applied to the county for a use variance. The neighbors fought it and won. The parties are gone and the house sits empty. Poor planning.

Are there plans to rezone in the near future? Have any contractors proposed new developments? We were shocked by a large rural housing development going up approximately 15 miles from where we live. If we had been a neighbor, we would have been upset.

Many counties offer tax deferrals for agricultural and forest use (to name a couple). A specified amount of acreage must be held and used for the primary purpose of growing and harvesting trees of a marketable species, or used primarily as farmland. You must often meet a certain economic threshold in the specific use to acquire lower taxes on your property. Find out the exact requirements before you purchase, as counties will retro-actively assess taxes if you neglect to meet the requirements. Sometimes you can convince the landowner to pay for the removal of tax-deferral designation before you purchase the land, but it can be quite expensive and most sellers refuse to remove it. Taxes on 20 acres may be consid-erably higher than on a small city lot, so avoid sticker-shock and obtain details on annual tax assessments. What criteria does the tax assessor use? Are the assessments up-to-date? Some are only updated when properties are sold. Some friends' taxes quadrupled with the new tax assessment. Some locations only allow taxes to go up a certain percentage each year. Additionally, insurance rates can skyrocket if fire stations are far away. Whether the fire stations are volunteer or staffed full-time affects rates. We experienced some surprise with our rates. Outbuildings, pools, and general umbrella policies can add up.

Financing Your Property

Seller financing is often a superior option for both the buyer and seller. You typically pay the seller a down payment and then make regular payments with a set interest rate. Many banks will not lend on older mobile homes, so seller financing may be the only option. If you enter into seller financing, verify that you get all terms in writing and obtain a title search so you know about any liens, encumbrances, or easements on the property. Make certain you clarify if the seller can sell the mortgage; what happens if he/she

Unusual properties may need creative financing.

passes away; if there are any pre-payment penalties; and other matters potentially causing problems in the future.

When using a commercial lender ask about the various loan programs. Check out banks, mortgage companies, and credit unions, as they carry different types of loan programs. Loans and programs exist to assist specific types of people or specific types of land. Mention if you are a first-time homebuyer, a veteran, or hoping to buy a farm. Some programs assist with down payments or construction. On larger pieces of property, you may find it difficult to obtain a mortgage. We had to go through a mortgage company with a division specializing in properties over 20 acres.

If you purchase raw land, determine if you want to build it yourself or hire a general contractor. That decision influences loan availability, the length of time to pay it back, and the interest rates. The more unconventional your property, building, or remodeling scheme, the more time you should allot to acquiring a loan. If you own a small business, or buy something off-grid, such factors make it even more complicated. Accumulate as large a down payment as possible.

A number of friends live on off-grid properties and each of their financial and loan situations differ significantly. One family obtained a short-term, low-interest loan on their raw property. Once their home was built, they would roll the loan into a conventional loan. At the end of the term, their home stood incomplete. Their lender did not know how to evaluate their partially finished home or compare it with other properties. An incomplete, remote, off-grid property did not fit within any of their normal lending parameters. The same lender eventually offered a new loan to the family, in part, we suspect, because it could not imagine foreclosing on such an unusual property.

The more unique your property or the plans for your homestead, the more challenges you may find with financing and construction. Do your homework, plan ahead, and boost your chances for success!

https://goo.gl/YEMXXz

Mrs. Wranglerstar holds a blacksmith-forged garden fork.

Stewardship

There's no reason not to start something just because it's a big job. When we first purchased the homestead, we were discouraged by how the previous owners had left the land. They had taken, but they didn't give anything back, and they left the property neglected. We were intimidated by the scope of work we had to do, but we started by limbing just one tree. Then we realized that this is our life's work — God put our family here for a reason. Perhaps it was to teach us stewardship.

God speaks to us through His creation. I understand the excitement of the city, but everything there is created by human hands, as if to say, "Look what man has created." By being in the country, we see something else. We see things God created, which brings our thoughts higher. We can glorify the things that come from the hands of the Creator, rather than the hands of humans. There are benefits to being a good steward of the land, and God speaks to us through that.

Some people watch the Wranglerstar videos and complain that we're not environmentally friendly because we cut down trees. However, that's simply not true. They object when we cut down trees and use chainsaws, but they misunderstand what it means to be good stewards. Being good

stewards is not about eating at the greenest restaurants, driving a green car, or wearing environmentally friendly clothing. Think of the impact we leave when we cut down our own timber compared to the impact involved when buying lumber from chain stores.

Right now, we're focusing on leaving this place better than it was than when we came. In the forests, we're limbing up trees and thinning out the smaller ones. This will allow the healthy trees to grow, and it will prevent wildland fire hazards. Although some people fear that cutting down trees is bad for the environment, part of good forest stewardship involves thinning out unhealthy trees and allowing the best ones to grow. While we don't take cutting down trees lightly, trees are meant to be used. We don't let the trees go to waste though. Here are just a few ways that we try to use every part of the trees we cut down:

- Mill the main part of the trunks for timber
- Chop the smaller portions into firewood

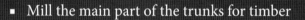

Lumber Bought at Chain Stores
Heavy equipment burning diesel in the forests
Vehicles driving to and from the forests
Log trucks transporting the wood across the country
Power bill to run the store

Timber from the Homestead
A few gallons of chainsaw gas
Short distance from the forest to where the timber will be used

- After we burn the firewood, we use the ashes to fertilize our garden and orchard and to repel bugs

- Pile up the smaller limbs to dry and chip for mulch or leave the piles in the forest to make habitats for animals

- Gather and bag the sawdust for composting or cleaning up spills

- Collect the scraps of wood for kindling and fuel for our blacksmith forge

Using every part of the tree is all part of God's plan for our stewardship of His creation. It's certainly not wasteful, and it even leaves a smaller environmental impact than if we bought the wood from chain stores. We realize that we have a big task ahead of us in terms of rehabilitating our property, but we can't wait to see where God will teach us through this process.

Cody's chainsaw mill is convenient to use in the woods and in the shop.

Checking the wood
cut and grain

4

Chickens Come Home to Roost

At Noble Valley, as we worked fervently to beat the end of the season, we received an enormous blow. It was on a Monday in mid-August. The concrete was scheduled for delivery when the contractor called to confirm the price. The foundation should cost around $20,000. The quote came in at over $80,000. This completely gutted our budget, decimating our plan to finish construction out of pocket. We were stunned and felt in a bit of a frenzy with winter approaching and not enough money to build. We lacked both permanent and temporary quarters for our housing and our business.

Posing with one of our fifth wheels.

We needed a plan of attack. And we needed it quickly. I spent Tuesday and Wednesday on the phone with banks and other commercial lenders. We sought to obtain a loan to complete our house and shop. The more we spoke with loan officers, the more the property seemed too unusual (too far out of town, off-grid, surrounding property valued too low, fire department too far away) for a bank to give us a loan.

Thursday we met with the engineer to discuss possible changes to decrease the cost of the foundation. We hoped that with our suggested changes, the amount of concrete for completion would be substantially less. Because of the extremely rough road and long distance out of town, there were few companies even able to bid on our project. With directions given to our engineer, we now had to wait for his results before we could request resubmittals for the bids on the foundation work. He assured us he would have the answers by Monday. It was certain to be the longest weekend ever.

Dumbfounded, we had a physical and emotional desire to do something, anything. Because it was irrational to dump more time and money into developing the property until we obtained the results from the engineer and received updates from the mortgage loan officers, we hit the road to check out properties fitting our tightening budget. While this seems like an about-face, and we likely qualified for a loan, we were concerned we would not be able to pay it back in the foreseeable future. With our move to such a remote location, we knew we were going to take a huge hit to our income. We were willing to submit to the hit, but only if the mortgage on the raw land was our only debt. In good faith, we could not take on the additional debt of a construction loan at that point. We did not want to set ourselves up for future failure.

We drove around and found ourselves back in the same area as those properties we looked at three years earlier. While we wanted to use the same stringent criteria as in our initial search, our current situation had changed substantially and many more properties emerged as viable options. This was not because more properties were available, but because we could no longer be as fussy. We were no longer living the dream; we were facing a stark reality.

As we headed to one parcel Friday afternoon, we passed a property with a for sale sign. We stopped and looked around. It had not appeared online. It sparked my interest. I wrote down all the facts I could find and we drove on to the place we had initially come to visit, which happened to be the closest neighbor. The owner was home and showed us the multiple outbuildings, an older home, and luxurious gardens. While we liked the property, I found myself sneaking in questions regarding the property down the road. As we left, Cody gave me the "absolutely not" talk. The house down the road had a million and one things wrong with it, and

Our first view of homestead

Condition of homestead and garden when we purchased it

that was only what we could see on the outside. The price was also likely more than we would qualify for with a mortgage.

The next day we headed out again, with similar results, several lovely houses and properties, but none felt like our potential home. At the end of the day I asked Cody to drive 45 minutes out of our way to check out the "absolutely not" house again. He gave me "that" look, but honored my request. Invoking common sense, he noted it was quite far out of town, the area suffered high snow accumulation, the growing season was likely short, and we would be buying a property in which every square inch would again require remodeling, including the outbuildings. He dismissed my favorable impressions toward the land and buildings. The stunning view he could not deny. We started our two-hour drive back to our undeveloped property, the fifth wheel, and a barrage of facts and emotions.

On Sunday, Cody's parents accompanied us through backcountry roads, in houses charming or pitiful, past barns made of cargo containers, mountains majestic, and barking dogs. The last stop of the day was the "absolutely not" house. We again drove substantially out of the way to arrive there. Upon approaching, Cody uttered the word I wanted to hear, "Maybe." I knew it could be ours.

When we arrived, the former owner of the home was there emptying it of her belongings. Unfortunately, her family had suffered hardship and was losing the place in foreclosure. It was a calamitous and common reality in both the early 2000s and in many rural communities. It benefitted us because properties far out of our financial reach three years earlier were now within grasp. This home fell into that category — financially reasonable and rural enough that exceedingly few people wanted to live "way out there." She graciously showed us through the house and answered multiple questions. She expressed contentment in knowing her family's loss might be our gain. While she wished they could remain there, she understood they could not and hoped someone "worthy" could be stewards of the place in their stead. We thanked her and took our leave. Much discussion was held in the van. We knew we would be hearing from the engineer in the morning.

To Stay or Not to Stay

Monday arrived and with it the engineer's report on our foundation. We had prayed fervently that the Lord would give us a clear answer on whether we should move forward with building on the mountain at Noble Valley or pull the plug. He did not. The engineer told us he changed the shape of some walls and adjusted the requirements for the foundation to comply with our county's codes, instead of the urban codes upon which he made the original calculations. The concrete requirement would now be less than a quarter of what been required in our initial bid specifications.

We contacted the firms and asked for new bids. Over and over again "$20,000." $21,000." $20,500." Exactly the amount we originally budgeted for the foundation. Should we continue building? Even though our finances were now back on track, we came to realize exactly how expensive it would be to live on the mountain property and how ill-equipped our living situation would be. It was much more than we had thought. Realistically, we could no longer afford to move there. Yes, Cody could secure an office or construction job somewhere. I could go back to work. We could put Jack in school and daycare. We could afford to build a house and live on the mountain then, but we had moved there precisely not to live that lifestyle.

The thought of pulling up stakes and starting over was heartrending. We had already invested thousands of dollars and countless hours clearing timber, building roads, and installing a septic system and fresh-water well. We had fallen in love with our future home site and developed relationships with neighbors persisting to this day. We faced a dreadfully difficult decision. Should we continue to bang our heads against the proverbial wall or cut our losses, take the remaining money, and use it as a down-payment on a property with an intact infrastructure?

Frustration in the fifth wheel

"Bingo" is a term used by pilots. It is the amount of fuel necessary for a pilot to abort his flight plan and still return to a safe, reliable landing spot. When the winner of the game shouts "bingo," the game is over. Similarly,

"Pride goes before destruction, and a haughty spirit before a fall" (Proverbs 16:18).

when gas levels dictate a flight is over, "bingo" has been reached. It is the final reserve. We reviewed numbers and interest rates, prayed, poured over paperwork, and stared at the stack of permitting we had completed for Noble Valley. We reviewed the bid numbers repeatedly. Cody looked at me and said, "I think we've hit bingo." I cried and cried and cried. Cody got angry. Not mean-angry but sad-angry. No-answer-to-the-dilemma-we-were-in angry.

We dropped Jack off with grandparents while we sorted out our future. And cried. And talked. And wrestled with God. Earlier that week I had sent Cody an email and included this *"Unless the LORD builds the house, they labor in vain. . . . It is vain for you to rise early, to sit up late, to eat the bread of sorrows; for He gives His beloved sleep"* (Psalm 127:1–2). It seemed far too apropos.

We wanted to wallow but simply did not have the time. We decided to purchase the "absolutely not" property. For a million and one reasons, we knew it was a better choice for us, but it was humbling. Truly humiliating to be unsuccessful at such a project. We were swept up in calls and meetings and paperwork, wrapping up obligations at Noble Valley, and getting an offer together on the homestead. Despite this busyness, it was a dark time. We refused to accept that the Lord caused any of our hardship at Noble Valley, for when we prayed, we realized we had resisted His guidance on many things. Noble Valley had been a three-year detour and we were now back on track. Admittedly, our pride was hurt too. *"Pride goes before destruction, and a haughty spirit before a fall"* (Proverbs 16:18). I do not think we can overstate how difficult this time was for us.

We were still headed in the right direction, following our dreams, endeavoring to move toward a homestead, toward spending our time together. When we take risks, we are not assured success, but a life without risks would be one of regrets. I doubt most misgivings derive from what people do, but rather from what people were too afraid to do. I can recall times when the Lord wanted us to act but it seemed too difficult. I regret those missed opportunities. I do not regret Noble Valley.

Completely distorting a quote I read once, what if historical figures of the past feared to explore lands not yet seen, terrified that the world really was flat, considering the security of their retirement and worrying they might get hurt along the way? What if our heroes hid at home? What if we allow greed, corruption, and evil to rule, to win? What if our mistakes were limited to what was the right shade of beige to paint our homes? Where would we be if we never risked it all? Articles circulate about being a "yes" rather than a "no" parent. However, I want more; I want to be a "yes" person, not just parent. Certainly, bills must be paid and duties fulfilled, but does the perfect lawn outweigh looking at clouds with a child? Why is making money at a stress-filled job more important than eating popcorn on the couch while creating bad jokes? Who created these "rules" and why do so many of us follow them? Why do we not say yes to taking a chance?

I know a family where fear dictates. None of them wants the life they are living. The security has become stifling. The children burst from their safety. They are on the edge of something beautiful. It may not be all uphill and victory, but one can see their aspirations alight, the call to take the chance. The risks are worth it.

Not for Sale

And with that we decided to purchase the "absolutely not" homestead. First, we needed to determine if it was even available, as it was not recorded on the local real estate listing service. We left a message for the seller's real estate agent telling her we were considering making an offer on the property. In taking this step, we were completely closing the door on continuing to build on the Noble Valley property. Even if we were unable to purchase the homestead, we knew we must rent or buy something else. Soon.

The realtor called to report the homestead sold at a foreclosure auction only two days earlier back to the bank. Thrilled, supposing the bank would want to dispose of the empty home quickly, we made an offer. Unbelievably, the new realtor refused to present our offer to the bank. She claimed paperwork and getting the property "ready" would take a week or so and then the bank wanted to close within 45 days but would prefer 30. This would put our move-in date around the end of September. We could continue to store our tools and equipment at Noble Valley and in our seven storage units. Cody could maintain his business in his ad hoc way. We could live in the fifth wheel. One more month of expenses and inconveniences sounded bearable.

In reality, the seller's realtor would not even present our offer until the end of September. Now this caused a problem. The fall rains swamped our off-grid property and made the treacherous road conditions both muddy and treacherous. We had two fifth wheels, my vehicle, Cody's truck and tools, and other items at Noble Valley. After a weekend of rain, I struggled but got my vehicle out, but not the four-wheel drive truck. It took three days of the sun baking the ground hard enough to drive on before it could escape. The fifth wheels threatened to lodge permanently in the ground. We found an RV park, but the longer Cody limped along without a dedicated business location, the less we wanted to spend. We started selling everything we owned: bikes, stand-up paddleboards, toys, stocks, dirt bike gear, and finally, the excavator. We knew we wanted the excavator on the homestead, but we needed a down payment more.

We had to sell everything, including our excavator, for a down payment on the homestead.

The morning the homestead finally listed, three offers rolled in. We made a full price offer in as-is condition. The other two ended up being low-ball offers. Incredibly, our offer was not accepted. The bank's out-of-state representative counteroffered for $1,000 over

asking price and a list of adden-
dums over which we either had no
control or made no sense, such as
paying a daily fee if the bank failed
to adhere to the contract, thus
delaying closing. Strange, yes? This
was only the start of plentiful delays
and unimaginable requests too
numerous to list.

Stuck in the mud

The lender required two separate
approvals — the property and us.
We were not the problem. The
property needed to be worth as
much as the agreed sales price. A
neutral third-party appraiser valued
the homestead at significantly less than we offered. As standard industry
practice, the lender would only loan 80 percent of the appraised amount,
not the agreed sales amount. The representative threatened to terminate
the contract because the house no longer qualified for financing for the
agreed amount. Because of the low appraisal and new negotiations on
price, the lender needed to review and rewrite financing paperwork,
and the time set to close extended. The representative refused to grant
an extension unless we again agreed to pay a daily fee. The low appraisal
price was not our fault, so we lost even more days explaining to the
representative why we would not pay a fee.

We were now looking at a late October closing date despite submitting
an offer in August. We still lacked a home. The homestead house and
outbuildings stood empty and we were miserable. We received permission to pull our fifth wheel into an almost empty parking lot — railroad
tracks on one side and highway on the other. Not ideal, but the price was
free. We could also stay at Cody's parents' vacation rentals when they
were empty. Cleaning them to hotel standard was our payment. Great
deal. The rentals were much nicer than the parking lot, but staying for a
short time and then cleaning to vacation rental cleanliness and lugging
things from rental to fifth wheel to rental wore us down. While we were
thankful for the generosity we received, it was a difficult time. No home.
No idea if we were going to acquire the property we wanted. Not positive
if we should rent another shop for Cody, which meant no stable income.

We were also questioning if we made the correct decision. In hindsight, we believe the Lord was seeing whether we were going to follow His lead or push ahead with our own schemes again. We were called to trust and remain patient. We both are terribly (and terrifically) independent and motivated. Like any trait, these can be a blessing or a curse. We were physically and emotionally distraught. I will spare you more details, but I do not recall that time with any fondness.

To add to our burdens, because of the substandard quality of comparable properties in the area, the low appraisal value, and the dreadfully destitute condition of the homestead, the underwriter required a second appraisal and a field review (critique of the first appraisal). The review would not only cost us money, but time. It was already late October and these were some of the longest months of our lives. Unfortunately, this required asking the representative for another extension of time. He refused unless we paid $2,500. We refused. The property stood unoccupied and neglected. It had been on the market over a year and a half in a remote location. Buyers would be few. Its inability to pass muster could not be blamed on us. About an hour before the sales contract would expire and we would be unable to recuperate our earnest money, we terminated the contract. It was not a happy day.

 https://goo.gl/twiFTm

Questioning our decision

Wisdom from the Journey

Do You Even Want to Move to the Country?

When considering moving to the countryside, there are many things to consider. Foremost, do you really want to move out of the city?

Who Wants to Move?

If you are part of family, does the entire family want to move? The entire family might be gung-ho to move to the country but with distinct expectations. One person might be willing to buy land without an access road, camp in the snow, and simply see what odd jobs come along in order to pay future costs. The other might want a newly built house, desiring a stable income source and living on a paved road so help can come if necessary. Both fit in the rural landscape and lifestyle. Neither is better than the other is, but age, gender, skill level, and previous experiences influence what is crucial to feel comfortable and secure at home. Cody and I always preferred properties where you cannot see another neighbor. Most people consider us crazy, because they want to be able to see another house; they deem line of sight as somehow safer. Exciting or frightening might be used to describe the exact same situation. A 17- and 70-year-old undoubtedly consider skydiving, traveling around the world by bike, or moving to the country very differently.

How Far Out of Town?

Do not move to a remote location if one spouse lacks enthusiasm. Even if the reluctant one never complains, it is easier on a marriage to find a compromise. Would moving far away diminish or harm relationships with family or friends? This consideration undoubtedly kept us closer to Portland than if family lived elsewhere. Fortunately, our move put us closer to Cody's sister and her husband, with whom we love to spend time. If you love your social organization, church group, or are a gym rat, and now live 45 minutes away (in fair weather), it might be difficult to be involved regularly. One friend bought a property only 15 minutes out of town, but still laments she lives too far. Between driving the children to school and activities, and her husband's in-town business, even that commute has become burdensome.

Older children's involvement in activities and school might bring up issues as you consider where to locate. Will your children attend public school, private school, or homeschool? At 6:55 each morning our public school bus drives by, yet school does not start until 8:15. Would you want your children to spend that much time riding back and forth each day? Friends live roughly 25 minutes away from the nearest school bus stop. That stay-at-home mother typically drives two hours a day in order for her children to catch the bus. At first glance, these commutes sound awful, however, time spent commuting can be both relaxing and an opportunity to communicate with family or friends. We know one homeschooling family whose children played soccer on the public school team each weekday and on weekend game days. The drive provided the teenagers and parents a lot of one-on-one time to talk, which otherwise may not have occurred so regularly.

What Can You Afford?

Not what do you want to be able to afford, but what does your budget truly allow? Make certain to bear in mind emergencies: cars stop functioning; arms and legs break, roofs leak. Pay off your debt. Establish a savings account. If it is tight, wait. I definitely wish we had. The excitement of owning rural property quickly diminishes when something derails the financial plan.

Friends purchased a raw piece of land ten years ago. Five years later they moved, with their two small children, into an "uninsulated shell of a house," lacking plumbing and electricity. The house sits atop of the garage so they ran up and down stairs to use the outhouse. Another five years passed, and they now boast insulation, a large generator, wood stove, four-burner gas range, and a toilet upstairs. They still lack plumbing and electricity so must climb the stairs to turn on the generator to power their computers and lamps. They use a cooler they fill with ice, stopping at their refrigerator and freezer in a storage unit, 30 minutes away, to stock up on food. They hope for running water and a sink soon — lugging water has become tedious: "Laundry is done at either the laundromat or a family/friend's house — hand washed here if we're in a pinch. Water is heated in a big stockpot on the wood stove for dishes and baths. Dishes are done in two tubs (dirty and clean) on the kitchen table."

This was not their plan. The plan was to build more quickly. The wife confesses they were naïve, imagining they would finish the house in 18 months, then five years. Now she jokingly suggests the house will be complete in 15. She would do it again, but admits she misses some everyday basics, "Warm water that comes out of a faucet" and "the fridge, washer, and dryer — I really want those!" We met one couple who lived in a basement for over five years. They wanted no debt so never obtained a small construction loan. Count the cost before moving!

How Much Land Can You Take Care of?

Our first yard measured the standard 50' x 100' city lot and never looked great. Granted, we both worked more than full-time, were remodeling the house, and I was pregnant or with a newborn in my arms. Our second yard was an acre and a half and provided plenty to do. It possessed five huge apple trees, a real waterfall, shops, raised garden boxes, berry bushes, and an enormous yard to mow. Raking took a full day or two. I suspect an acre or two would satisfy most people. You can raise animals, plant an enormous garden, and tend a little orchard on a few acres — big enough you might even acquire a pond or stream.

Generally, if you buy a smaller property, fewer tools and machinery are necessary. We reside on over 50 acres, and while we save for a tractor and riding mower, we use a small second-hand push mower and borrowed walk-behind mower, building muscle. Because of the yard's size, to keep fire danger at bay and to look fairly reasonable, we must put it into a mowing rotation. Friends bought sheep for that purpose, but then you own animals to tend, and butcher . . . but I digress.

Take into Account the Weather

Consider not only if the climate is suitable for growing your own food but other projects your property will demand. Sunshine or rain? Opportunity to try a new climate? We moved from rain and wet to snow and sun. Thrilled! However, our growing season shortened dramatically. In Portland, in the Willamette Valley, you grow fruits and vegetables even

if you do not intend to do so. It is ridiculously easy to cultivate and grow plants there. Here, we must plan and be diligent concerning gardening, because of our short season. It was quite an adjustment.

One high-elevation, remote-living friend told me, "We basically have a three-month weather window in which anything related to outdoors — firewood, road work, clean up, excavating, concrete, etc. — all has to get done. And usually one month of that window is restricted by fire danger. That is also the time when [my husband] does a lot of side work making money to pay for the larger projects around the property."

Our vehicle during winter at our homestead

Do You Like the Impression the Neighborhood Gives?

Find a suitable community before you look for your new home or property. Land may be cheap in a certain area, but if you dislike the area or it does not meet your criteria, then the cost may be irrelevant. There is a location, roughly an hour from where we live, that we kept trying to make ourselves love. We spent a lot of time there, because the prices were great. Unfortunately, we simply did not want to live there. Driving a few miles in either direction can dramatically change the neighborhood. Remember that in the country you will always be a newbie, even after living there for 20 years.

Rural customs do not change especially quickly, so make sure you can live with them. Status quo has an inertia difficult to dislodge.

If all of the houses appear shabby, disassembled cars stand mounted on concrete blocks in the yard, and growling dogs pull on the end of chains, will you want to live there? Will you feel safe going for a walk? If your neighbor owns five goats and 25 chickens despite the urban zoning, will you care? In a large number of rural communities, business, farming, forestry, and residential uses mix harmoniously. Anticipate a farm on one side, a carpenter on another, and a car mechanic on the other. Will that bother you? All 50 states, and numerous rural communities, mandate the "right to farm," which protects farms and ranches from those who complain about their activities. Generally, this means if a farmer must operate equipment and machinery all night to harvest crops, they can. Your right to peace and quiet is secondary. Furthermore, this mandate may allow the spraying of chemicals you might find offensive; the burning of slash piles, fields, and ditches creating smoke; and the production of manure.

Maybe you love a neighborhood because its character seems so rural, yet also feels manicured and well-kept. To some people's surprise, large acreages can also be part of a homeowners association. We belonged to one where each parcel averaged over 20 acres. Make sure you agree with the tenets; some dictate the size of the homes and preclude building guest-houses and adding extra outbuildings. Associations regularly establish use and maintenance agreements concerning wells and private roads.

When you move to the country, it is tough to be totally self-reliant. You will likely be called upon to volunteer in some capacity. Whether this means helping with the local farmers' market, volunteer fire department, or sports programs, you need your community and it needs you. One neighbor automated most things: chickens and turkeys receive fresh water, the coop door opens at dawn and closes at dusk, his cattle's water is heated, and his thermostat keeps his house at a consistent temperature. This is not the norm. Usually if you want to leave for a time, your neighbors feed your critters, water your orchard and garden, and double-check everything looks buckled down if the weather changes. Additionally, it is nice to stop in for a cup of coffee, obtain a little advice, and see a friendly face.

Now erected in plenty of areas, large windmills can be noisy and either visually fascinating or marring, depending upon your point of view. Is there a rural airport close by? Do the dusters leave early in the morning to spray fields? Noise can be a burden or a comfort. One friend reported to me she hates "just how quiet it really is." Peaceful for a short while, she now misses the city's constant background noise.

Rent or Lease

Try out rural life. Leasing allows you to observe an area before you commit. Renting can be more inexpensive than buying, which might allow you to move to the country before you acquire a down payment. Purchasing a piece of property is a hefty investment. Additionally, rural real estate can be tougher to sell if you realize it is not for you. There are more buyers for a house in the city than in the country. The first house we seriously looked at in the country remains for sale, seven years later. The land is wonderful, the house is impeccably built, and no one has bought it because it is so remote.

Renting lets you meet people in the community who can inform you about available property that never hits the commercial real estate market. When people know you, they may make a better deal with you or consider owner financing. Additionally, many farmers and ranchers gladly trade work for a place to stay. You not only get to live rurally but you receive an education in animals and farming too.

https://goo.gl/bsv9vf

How to Cut Firewood

Learning to cut firewood is not only a fantastic form of exercise, but will help you thin out unhealthy trees and allow the best ones to grow. Additionally, it is an abundant, renewable energy source that usually costs less than oil and natural gas for heating purposes. A cord of wood is a stack of wood measuring 4 feet by 4 feet by 8 feet. When skilled, you can cut a couple of cords a day. Wood provides a delightful heat and an ambiance which can't be beat.

Felling and bucking with a cross-cut saw is wonderful, but today most firewood is felled, bucked, and split using more modern tools. No matter what tools you use, make certain to think about safety first and not to overwork your body. Accidents often happen when you are fatigued.

WHAT YOU'LL NEED:

- Chainsaw — For the first-time buyer, I'd recommend a medium-sized saw, like the Husqvarna® Rancher or the Stihl® Farmboss. For what you get, these saws are an excellent value.

- Wood splitter — It's possible to split your wood by hand; however, if you have over three cords of wood to split, consider purchasing a hydraulic wood-splitter.

- Safety equipment — Be sure to wear safety goggles, earplugs, faller chaps, and leather gloves for protection.

- Faller's belt — Keep your tools handy while felling and bucking by storing your ax and falling wedges in a faller's belt.

- Small ax — one 2.5–3 lbs. with a 26-inch handle.

- Falling wedges — Two to three. I prefer plastic.

- Pickeroon — This tool is a great backsaver.

INSTRUCTIONS:

- Select your tree. Trees that are dead, dying, or with defects should be cut first. *Tip: Smaller trees make good firewood because they don't require splitting. Larger branches are exceedingly dense, generating more BTUs when burned.*

- Determine which way you want the tree to fall based on the direction the tree is leaning and other objects or trees in the area.

- Cut a wedge out of the side of the tree in the direction you want it to fall. For example, if you want the tree to fall to the south, cut the wedge on the south side of the tree.

wranglerstar.com videos

Real Environmentalists Cut Down Trees

Real Environmentalists Cut Down Trees 2

The Giving Tree

Felling Giant Trees

- Begin cutting horizontally on the opposite side of the tree, but don't cut all the way through.

- Hammer the falling wedges into the horizontal cut with the back end of the ax. Make sure the area where the tree will fall is clear. The pressure from the wedges will cause the tree to fall.

- Limb up the fallen tree by cutting off all the branches. Start on one end and work your way down, cutting the branches as close to the trunk as possible on all sides.

- Clean up the limbs and place them in a pile to the side. *Tip: Clean up each tree as you go to keep the area neat and clear of debris.*

- Cut the tree into rounds, approximately 16–24 inches.

- Move the wood splitter close to the rounds. Stick the pickeroon into the top of two rounds; place one on the wood splitter and lay the other aside for quick access. *Tip: Create an efficient workflow by splitting two rounds at a time. While one is splitting, have the other ready to go when the first one is done.*

- Remove the pickeroon from the top and use it to guide the round while it is splitting.

- Split the round according to its size — sometimes splitting it in half works, but other times it's best to split it into quarters.

- After the first two rounds are split, load up the wood and repeat the process until all the rounds are split and loaded. *Tip: Make sure the firewood is dried and cured before burning. Firewood dries from the ends, about one inch per year. Store the wood in a dry, well-ventilated place to cure.*

- Finish cleaning the area by "mushrooming" the stump. Cut off the edges of the stump in thin strips by cutting in a circular motion around the stump. This will make the stump look more natural and will prevent future damage.
- Prepare your equipment for its next use by refueling and oiling the saw and splitter, blowing out the saw's air filter, and sharpening the saw chains.

5

What Have We Done?

After enduring so much, we could not believe we no longer had a contract to purchase the homestead. The hours leading up to terminating the contract were some of the most tense of our lives. Emails, texts, and faxes flew between our agents. In hindsight, the bank representative had been playing games the entire time. An unsuccessful sale did not genuinely affect him.

Finally, we're at home!

One point Cody and I were certain about was we wanted to live in the community where the homestead was located. It was the same area we had liked and seriously contemplated moving to years earlier, but had not. We felt fully convinced we would eventually live there. Therefore, while the house-purchasing shenanigans were occurring, we persisted in searching for properties for sale or for rent in the area. We did not locate adequate housing, but leased a shop for Cody a few miles from the homestead. We desperately required more income and wanted to become familiar with the area's inhabitants. The location was less than ideal, over an hour and a half each way from where we were living temporarily, but Cody continued to provide for us. We emptied several of the storage units and slowly got his new shop into working order. Jack and I would frequently go with him, likely not much help, but beneficial for us to share a common goal for those hours. On each trip, Cody and I would look at each other and confirm we wanted to live there.

After a short while, the representative granted an extension to our obtaining a field review and financing for a mortgage. We withdrew our termination. No appraisers in the area consented to conduct a field review, as they did not want to offend the first appraiser, likely a close colleague, and there was allegedly potential liability, both civilly and criminally. Our mortgage broker finally found an appraiser to perform a separate appraisal, but she refused to comment on the first appraisal. There were more delays, costs, and legal craziness, but basically, we were exhausted. In conclusion, we bought the homestead. Our loan officer said this was the most well-documented file he had ever compiled. Clearly not a compliment.

Mental challenges? Check. Physical challenges? Next.

Our Bugs and Dirt Now

In late November, we took possession of the property and moved in. In our minds, the homestead grew better each day, but we arrived to a closed-up, stinky old house with rough outbuildings. Somehow, we always manage to move during harsh, unrelenting weather. Apartment — April showers. City house — autumn's wind and sleet. Riverview — December's wintry frozen rain. Noble Valley — dust and baking, blazing July heat. The homestead — bitter cold with deep snow on the ground. Cody's Nana said it best, "If you want bad weather, ask when they plan to move."

The first appraisal had been so low, in part, because of the extreme "smell" of the house. We surmised sitting empty, animals had moved in and elected to do things better done outdoors. This meant we again lived in the fifth wheel as we made the house habitable. We tossed all of the carpet out of the upstairs windows to the waiting dumpster. Bleach became our sidekick. We scrubbed every wall, ceiling, floorboard, nook, and cranny. We painted the floorboards, as we could not yet afford carpet. Looking back, we should have painted everything prior to

The homestead right before we moved in

Pouring concrete to change the barn into a shop on the homestead

moving in, but we had been adrift for so long, we craved to be in a home. We were ready, even if the house was not. At least it was clean.

We bought good bones. That is how one politely says, "Wow, your house could truly benefit from a remodel." Some spaces have been touched, but the majority still waits for updates. Every window and door requires replacing. The attic and floorboards require more insulation. Much of the plumbing demands attention. The ceiling started leaking from the upstairs bathtub, and months later the kitchen wall began bubbling with water. Cody tore apart the upstairs bathroom wall to fix the leak. Evidence of the fix awaits our remodel of the outdated and worn bathroom. We painted over wallpaper (a temporary fix) and put in carpet upstairs, but the layout necessitates reorganization too. Only a few walls (and doors and windows) to move. Good bones. I lamented to one friend the state of the property we had purchased and he retorted, "Yeah, but Cody likes projects. What else would he do?"

In addition to the rugged state of the house, we had no heat or water. A significant problem for late November. Pipes had frozen and burst in the house. The well was not functioning. We were hopeful the problem did not lie between the well-house and home, as it was a quarter mile length of pipe under a decent amount of snow. The house had previously been heated by wood stove but the door was busted on the stove and the chimney was incomplete. No firewood remained. We purchased wet, uncured wood off Craigslist and found out the sellers had logged our very own property. Incredibly, the firewood came home. At a steep price. Snowy, cold winter days allow the free market to up the price!

One issue is undeniable — we suffered no boredom. There was plenty to do. As mentioned, one of the barns was converted into a shop for Cody's business. We tore out stalls, poured a concrete floor, and installed temporary lighting. We moved things from the newly rented shop to the newly converted barn. Cody toiled in his unheated outbuilding until his lips turned blue and his fingers no longer moved, then he retreated to the house to work on a warmer project. Eventually we installed a stove in his space, but the building is vast, without insulation, and it provided minimal warmth at best. The modest amount of heat began to melt the snow on the roof, causing condensation to drip in the interior of the building, ruining things stored in the shop. We hastily moved an enormous amount of objects to two of the rooms in the house, lest they be destroyed. The items continue to reside in the house; this temporary situation no longer feels temporary.

Ready or Not

As we took care of getting the house and shop habitable and functional, and kept the business running, we were hit with an ice storm unlike any other. In truth, we live high enough in elevation we accumulated fluffy white snow. Lower in elevation they received ice, causing them to lose power for many hours. It also caused a large amount

Irresponsible logging, prior to our purchasing the homestead, left part of the forest in ruins.

of trees to topple across roadways, effectively shutting down the area for a day or two. A domino effect ended up knocking out our power, too — for eight days. We love camping and generally consider ourselves prepared for cold weather, but this experience opened our eyes to rural living. Between our lack of water and heat upon moving in, and now this, we were amazed at how dependent we had become on modern conveniences like warm water, a furnace with a thermostat, and grocery stores nearby. We had rushed to move in so the bulk of our belongings lay helter-skelter in various parts of the house and storage, to be sorted once spring and summer arrived. Now we were lamenting that decision since our generator and emergency supplies were hidden somewhere unknown to us. Our recent moves and lack of extra money precluded us from stocking a full pantry or freezer (in fact, we did not even own a refrigerator yet). Not being able to drive to town was a bit of a concern. We required more food, gas, and water. We found our generator amid our piles of belongings, but neglected to store extra gas on hand. We used the wood stove to cook and melt snow but we wanted a greater volume of water. Cody's business also demanded power in order to run our satellite dish for Internet and computers. We were not primed for an unpaid vacation yet. Our first venture down the road took us nearly twice as long as normal, but felt like a necessity.

Talk at the grocery store concerned how long we had gone without a proper shower and when we thought power would be restored. We quickly learned power outages were commonplace. Having no power was worn like a badge of pride the longer we went. Our elderly neighbor sat in our living room elated when our power switched on one evening. He rushed home to enjoy his own power once more. Sadly, he had to wait until the following day. Nine days and he won the hardship game in our neighborhood. Shortly thereafter, he put his house up for sale. He and his wife had enough. They were ready to move closer to town.

The adversities of our first winter were a blessing in disguise. We came face to face with the manifold shortcomings and assorted vulnerabilities in our preparations. It has been said every boxer has a plan until he is hit in the nose. Our noses had been bloodied and we resolved our second winter would not be a repeat of the first. *"My brethren, count it all joy when you fall into various trials, knowing that the testing of your faith produces patience. But let patience have its perfect work, that you may be perfect and complete, lacking nothing. If any of you lacks wisdom, let him ask of God, who gives to all liberally and without reproach, and it will be given to him"* (James 1:2–5). We needed a plan for future power outages and other emergencies. We knew it was not a matter of if, but when.

We frequently hear we are overdue for "The Big One," which in the Pacific Northwest means an earthquake of gargantuan proportions, potentially causing landslides, flooding, volcanic activity, and tsunamis on the coast. We live in "the ring of fire," surrounded by volcanos, some active and some lying in wait. In 1980, Mount St. Helens erupted, destroying everything in its wake and spewing ash farther than one could imagine. Authorities knew of the imminent eruption and issued evacuations. Even with such safeguards, 57 people died. Cody remembers the morning after, waking up to what, at first, looked like a snow day, but everything was a monochromatic color, with grey ash covering everything. Stores quickly sold out of painters' masks, aptly renamed "Mount St. Helens' masks." From our porch, we possess a stunning mountain view, surely giving us front row seats when it chooses to erupt. Beautiful and dangerous.

Our second winter

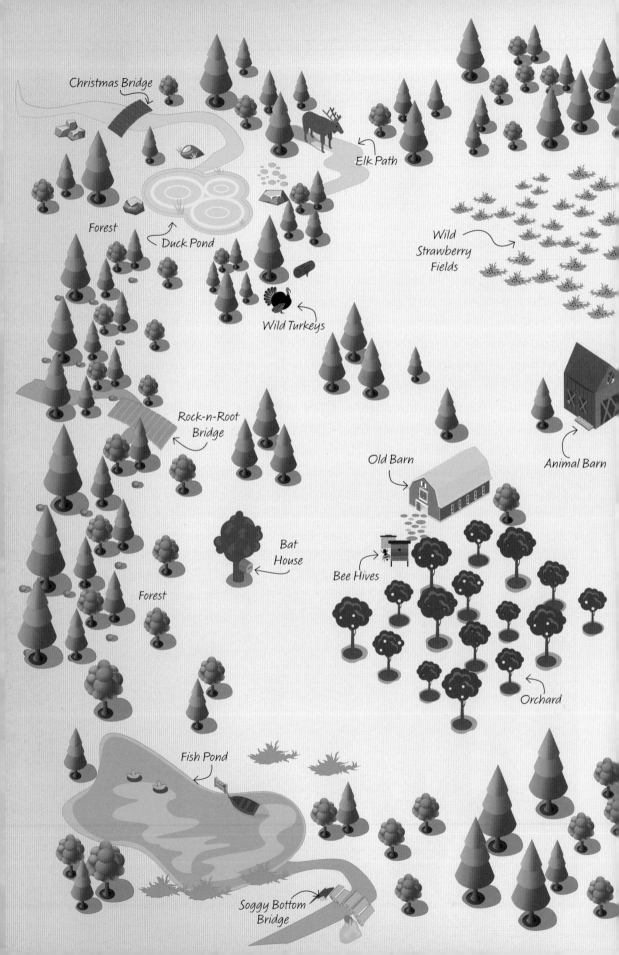

Christmas Bridge

Elk Path

Forest

Duck Pond

Wild
Strawberry
Fields

Wild Turkeys

Rock-n-Root
Bridge

Animal Barn

Old Barn

Bat
House

Bee Hives

Forest

Orchard

Fish Pond

Soggy Bottom
Bridge

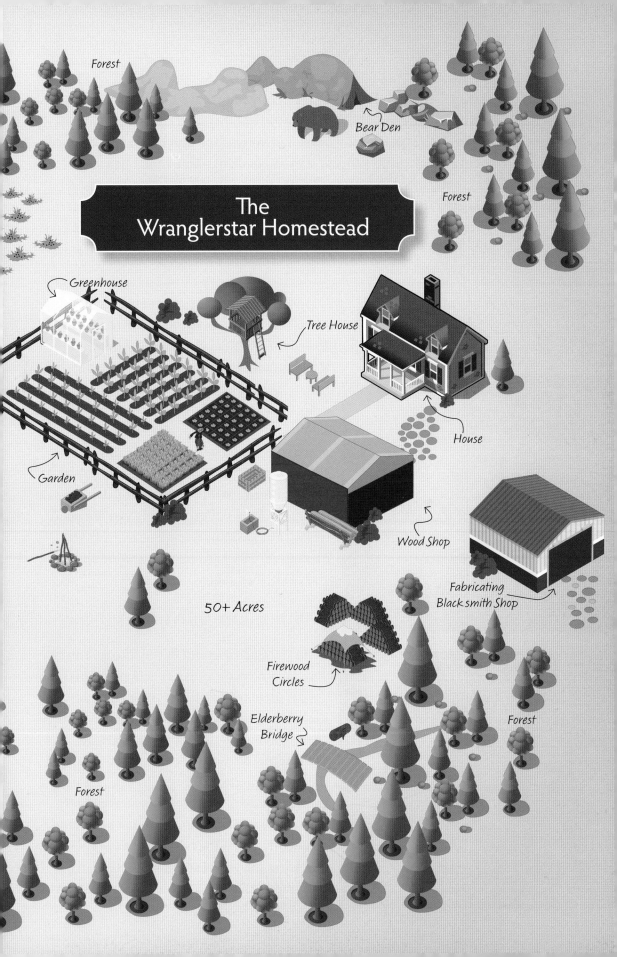

Our local and state authorities make themselves quite clear when the Big One occurs, cities will be taken care of first, then towns, and finally rural communities. The authorities advise that even city people should prepare to be "self-reliant" when it involves food and drink. City dwellers could enjoy a rustic, off-grid staycation of anywhere from one week to six months. That means, we, living rurally, must be prepared to sustain ourselves and cooperate with neighbors on our most pressing needs when such a time comes. Not to be scared, but prepared. Maybe that is why old-time farmers tend to save every board, nail, and wire, and stock a pantry with years' worth of food.

As we mulled over what was most vital for emergency preparedness, Cody brought up the four things one does if lost in the wilderness. It sounds silly but it concisely listed the essential elements of where to start: 1) build a shelter, 2) provide a source of heat, 3) secure water, and 4) find food. With a sturdy house and a dry roof, we moved to step two — provide heat and warmth. We had purchased a used woodstove and salvaged chimney pipe from the former stove and installed them. With perseverance, determination, and masses of exceedingly wet firewood we had a reasonably warm house. Next was making sure we had enough water, both hot and cold. Then food.

A ram pump became our solution.

The Drought

With the electricity out during the ice storm, the well pump no longer functioned. This meant no more water. We turned on our generator periodically and switched it from the well house to the hot water heater to the Internet to the lights and outlets. Eight days without the well pump had shown us how dependent we were upon conveniently available water. To plan to run the generator frequently, when the next emergency hit, was a less than ideal solution, particularly with the nearest gas station many miles away, down a dangerous ice-covered road. Not only did we want water, but hot water too. We found two interesting solutions. The first involved a better way of getting water. The second, how to heat water.

Vital water resources — efficiently used

A hydraulic ram pump is a water pump, which uses no electricity or solar power to move water. Instead, gravity and the kinetic energy of moving water provide the necessary energy. Water moves from an uphill source through a pipe to the ram pump, creating pressure, which redirects the water to the desired location. Later that spring, we constructed a ram pump to deliver water to my garden. The garden lay uphill from the ram pump, which delivered the water without difficulty. Efficiency was another factor. Nevertheless, it works. The short of the story is it is cheap to build, has only two moving parts, and uses no electricity.

Another alternative suggested to us repeatedly involved collecting water during rainfalls via gutters. However, tremendously heavy snowpack can accumulate at our elevation, so buildings tend not to have gutters, as they simply rip away from the roof. While there are other creative water solutions, we have not looked into other water catchment systems.

The hot water solution has yet to be implemented, but comes up in discussion occasionally. Heating water can be done by running a heat exchanger inside the firebox or chimney of a wood stove. The water flows through the pipes of the exchanger and gets heated as it runs through the hot wood stove. Hot water is thus available anytime the stove is running. We look forward to "free" hot water in the future. Friends report it is "fabulous," and everyone can take as long a shower as they like. One family ran the hot water under their floorboards for radiant heating, varying slightly from electric radiant heating. Apparently, that, too, is divine. Stories abound about using hot compost piles to heat water, but we have yet to see it in action.

https://goo.gl/sf7lxB

Wisdom from the Journey

What Skills Do You Possess?

Possessing a background in construction and site development, Cody was undaunted by the scope of work needing to be performed at our various properties. Clearing land, logging, construction, building roads, and installing septic systems and water wells were within his scope of abilities. If you cannot yet frame a wall, or plumb and wire a house, then starting with bare land will be exceedingly rough. It might be prudent to learn some of these skills on a more insignificant project than jumping in and being forced to live in . . . well, nothing, or an incomplete shack. Particularly if you have children.

Many a man has thought roughing it an adventure, while the wife has not fully embraced hovel (or worse) living. I do not intend to discourage taking a chance, but I do encourage being realistic about whether your entire family can handle the elements, deprivation, and hardship. It is tough to appreciate living cold, wet, and tired if you can easily remedy those hardships. Even Charles Ingalls moved his family into a house in town when winter proved powerfully cold and unrelenting. There is something to be said for hot baths, insulated walls, refrigerators, and doors on rooms. If you decide to move to a rural location, you would do well to possess or know the following.

Emergency Medicine

While you can get hurt anywhere, there seem to be many opportunities to do so in the countryside. Rusty nails go through boots and into feet, boys fall off trees, welders are burned, chainsaws slip hitting chaps but leaving major bruising, tools miss the mark cutting skin and dislocating bones. Ask us how we know. One cut necessitated seven stitches to Jack's forehead. While none of these accidents were life-threatening, getting an ambulance to our home would require at least a half-hour wait and such a rapid response would only occur if a volunteer were available immediately and close to one of the unmanned fire stations that serve our community. Our home's location necessitates we know basic first aid skills, as well as own a fully stocked first aid kit. You also want to be familiar with your emergency medical books. Figuring out how the books are laid out must be done before the emergency occurs.

Build a Reference Library

Get how-to books covering first aid, construction, plumbing, electrical, small engines, food preserving, and gardening. My father always said, "If you can read, you can do it." He knocked down walls, built walls, and knew when to call in a professional. He would say, "Just a minute," in a less than patient tone, when my brother and I interrupted him while he read up on how to wire electrical — one bit of construction he definitely wanted to get right! While we highly regard YouTube as a source to learn things, if the power is out, it is impossible to watch a how-to video on starting your generator. Additionally, if you find yourself in the attic dealing with leaky plumbing, a book might be easier (and more waterproof) to handle than a computer. Many good books can be picked up for a few dollars at garage sales, library sales, used bookshops, and thrift stores.

Basic Construction

It is invaluable to possess basic skills in plumbing, electrical, construction and wood framing techniques. While mastery of those skills is not necessary, you want to be able to deal with leaks, sparking outlets, and sagging walls safely and quickly. During a storm, ice may knock out your power while a tree careens through your roof. Your neighbors might be dealing with similar issues and the professionals might take days until they can help. While rural communities readily help one another, they assume that you can manage on your own while they take care of their own pressing needs first. Emergency services presume the same as well.

In addition to possessing basic skills, you also want to establish separate toolboxes for plumbing, electrical, and wood framing use. The toolboxes should include tools and how-to books, as well as fittings, wiring, screws, bolts, and nails for temporary use until you can secure items for permanent use. Keep a good selection of bungees, tarps, ratchet straps, and rope on hand as well. While this may sound silly, know how to use those things. Ratchet straps operate efficiently if you know how they work. If your knots are weak, you may lose a load.

Chainsaw Use

Unless you live in the desert or wide-open plains, you want to own a non-electric chainsaw and safety gear, and know how to use it under duress. Trees and their limbs fall across driveways and roads, and onto roofs. If you live remotely, you may even end up carrying a small chainsaw with you in your car during the stormy seasons. Chainsaws can be used to limb up trees to protect against fire danger, but also to trim back trees that may encroach close to power lines and homes. While a call to the power company may result in their trimming trees and limbs back from electrical lines, it can sometimes take a long time. Doing it yourself might keep the power on during a storm. You want non-electric because during emergency situations your power might be out, the electrical cord might not be long enough, and the cord always likes to get in the way.

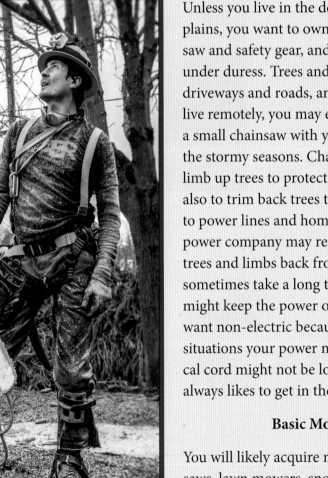

Basic Motor Repair

You will likely acquire many engines such as saws, lawn mowers, snow blowers, generators, tractors, and compressors. We have 12 small engines on our homestead. Each one requires unique filters, spark plugs, oil, etc. Every autumn each one must be winterized. Gas must be changed, because old gas can clog up filters and gas lines. Not only is there the initial investment in the purchase of the tool, but there is the cost to maintain those engines. Time expended to take care of these machines must also be taken into account. You should learn to adjust points, valves, carburetors, distributors, and spark plug gaps, and perform routine maintenance such as cleaning and oiling parts, and repair or replace defective parts such as water pumps, gears, pistons, and carburetors using hand tools. Additionally, you will likely tow larger loads once living rurally. Hauling large loads up hills can cause vehicles to overheat or strain axles; it is good to know what is an acceptable strain to put on your vehicle. If your vehicle does break down, it is a bonus to fix your car or truck enough to drive it to a repair shop instead of to pay for towing.

Along with basic repair, make sure all adults know how to use and fuel weather-related equipment. While Cody usually starts the generator, blows the snow, or runs the water pump, if he is gone, I need to know how to start and run these things. Some engines require mixed oil while others unadulterated oil. Our lawn mower and weed whacker do not use the same fuel. One wrong pour and engines are destroyed. Because wildland fires are a real threat, we own a water pump and tank located nearby to save the house and closest outbuildings if warranted. I do not use the pump, or engines in general, often enough to feel comfortable starting and running many of them. We devised a series of index cards with simple instructions that we attached to the pump. This way I can start and run the engine without ruining it (by letting it run dry). We practiced using the index cards so that in an emergency I can act

Mrs. Wranglerstar uses index cards to properly use the fire pump.

immediately, instead of trying to figure out what to do. While engines are second nature to Cody, they will likely always remain foreign to me.

Proper Weapon Use

Some people own guns but do not know how to use them properly. Learn how and practice frequently. One acquaintance shot a bullet through his living room chair. He thought it was unloaded. No one was hurt, but such an accident should never occur. Everyone should know an unloaded gun is to be handled with as much care as a loaded gun. I grew up without guns in the house, but when I met Cody, I realized guns would be part of my future home. Cody and I decided to attend numerous gun safety and use courses together. This way I would learn proper handling and safety techniques, and Cody would know my skill level.

Initially, I did not intend to carry a gun when I ran, as it was heavy and uncomfortable. When we first moved here, we walked in the forest west of our property and ran into our new neighbors. The petite woman, in her late 50s, wore a loaded revolver on an Alaskan guide chest harness. She told us about two separate experiences with bears in that very forest. One time her dog took after the bear. She stressed the importance of having a dog where we lived. While she clearly loves her dog, she realizes it is an essential tool in the forest, to allow her time and space to back away from wild animals. Our conversation with her made quite an impression. Cody and I made a compromise to buy an incredibly small gun I wear in backpack while running. It is not the perfect setup, but I have practiced its quick withdrawal, and it would sting more than a stone if I run into trouble. I also always run with our dog Lucy.

Cody and I deem it prudent to take a dog and firearm with us when we leave the yard surrounding our home and close outbuildings or when it is dark. Jack must keep a dog with him, even in broad daylight. He sticks close to home unless he is with a noisy bunch of children. We have spotted bear and coyote roaming in our pasture during the day and neighbors reported a mountain lion at our pond and in our pasture. The former owners kept their reindeer in our orchard area, protected by two great white Pyrenees. Only one night with the dogs gone and a mountain lion killed all of the reindeer.

In this past year alone, while running in the forests by our house, I encountered a black bear, a mountain lion, a bobcat, two foxes (not together), six coyotes (two separate occasions), skunk, badger, and came

Protection is a pet — Lucy running with Mrs. Wrangler.

across numerous deer, turkeys, pheasants, quail, owls, and snakes. That does not include what I spotted while in a car. While we have no desire to harm any animals unnecessarily, when I saw the bear, mountain lion, and coyotes, I called Lucy, prayed, pulled out my firearm, and waited. As they quickly retreated, so did my gun and I.

https://goo.gl/iIsKMu

Start Small and Start Today

Most people hear the term "homesteading" and think of 600 acres in the middle of nowhere. Not everyone is ready to move to the country or even convinced they need to. However, everyone can benefit from adopting a homestead philosophy or mentality to some degree. This is not to dissuade you from eating rice and beans for a year to save a down payment on a dream property, only encouraging you to start where you are. Urban and suburban homesteads may look a bit different but tend to engage the same ideas, simply scaled down a bit. Modern homesteading is often a way to think, and not just a way to live. It allows you to engage your community in a more personal manner. Below are some ideas to begin to embrace urban or suburban homesteading.

START A GARDEN. Whether this includes herbs grown in your kitchen window, small pots of tomatoes and cucumbers crowding your apartment balcony, or a plot in the local community garden or your back or front yard. When landscaping, choose to swap ornamental bushes and trees for fruit and nut-bearing varities. The amount of produce they bear might surprise you. The Dervaes family in California grows 6,000 pounds of produce on their 1/5 of an acre city lot (a fascinating family who have taken urban homesteading to the extreme with their 12 solar panels, composting toilet, chickens, and bees).

LEARN HOW TO COOK FROM SCRATCH. With produce and herbs from your garden, you are well on your way to more nutritious, tastier food. Although figures vary dramatically depending upon your source, the consensus is that freshly picked produced provides much more nutrition than that picked far away, shipped or trucked for days to weeks, stored in the back of the grocery, and then displayed for days before purchase. Apples and pears are stored up to a year before being sold.

LEARN BASIC MEDICINAL USES OF HERBS, VEGETABLES, AND FRUIT. While we are blessed to have year-round variety, shopping conveniences, and modern-day storage techniques, there is no denying fresh is best for the body. Most everyone has heard the saying, "Let food be thy medicine and medicine be thy food," attributed to Hippocrates. Yes, it's nice to have your own "farm-acy," and exciting to learn about the attributes of common foods. Garlic has antibiotic properties — use it for a mild earache before reaching for stronger antibiotics. For centuries, onions have been used to reduce inflammation and heal infections. The list goes on.

Wranglerstar:

The West Coast is the epicenter for the organic food movement. People are waking up to what they are putting in their bodies, what they're eating, and starting to figure out that local is usually better than they're getting at grocery stores.

PRESERVE YOUR FOOD. Learn to can, dehydrate, freeze, and ferment. Not only is it fun to use items you have grown or purchased, but tasty too.

MAKE YOGURT, KEFIR, AND CHEESE. They are easy to make and taste great.

RAISE CHICKENS, DUCKS, RABBITS, OR GOATS. Before you begin, you will want to check your municipal code and/or homeowner's association (HOA), as limits on the number and type of birds and animals are often specifically stated. Usually, roosters are not allowed because of their alarm-clock tendencies. Birds provide eggs and fertilizer (and sometimes meat) as well as help with tilling of garden beds and insect control.

KEEP BEES. Again, check your municipal code and HOA. Not only will your life be sweetened with honey, but your garden (and your neighbors') will benefit.

SAVE SEEDS. Let some of your plants go to seed or gather seeds from fruits and vegetables to grow the following year. Remember — you cannot collect seeds from hybrid plant varieties, only heirloom varieties.

THROW A SEED SWAP and/or food swap. One friend held a party where we brought home-preserved food, dried herbs, and extra seeds to swap. Make sure to label your items and use safe, tested recipes and include those with each item as well.

COLLECT RAINWATER and or greywater. Some communities prohibit this, but if not, set up a rain barrel to collect water from your gutters for your gardening needs. Greywater is water you've already used; so save the water from rinsing off your fruits and veggies, or draining your pasta, and use it to water your flowers and trees.

HANG YOUR LAUNDRY TO DRY. Not only do line-dried clothes and linens smell great but they offer savings as well.

PUT UP SOLAR PANELS. Many utility districts will pay or credit you for energy you produce. If you own a home, you can experiment with off-grid while remaining hooked to the grid.

INSTALL A WOODSTOVE. Woodstoves can be a delight to both cook on and heat your home. Unfortunately, many older models add to air pollution problems. Some communities ban installation of stoves completely or limit permitting to clean-burning, certified models. Annual fuel bills for woodstoves are less than both natural gas and oil, and cut down on nonrenewable fossil fuel use. Plus it will heat you thrice — once when cutting the wood on an out-of-town excursion, then when stacking it at home, and again when burning.

LEARN OTHER SKILLS. In the city, classes are offered on many topics from wood-working to blacksmithing to sewing and soap making, etc. While you may not have room for your own shop, you can frequently find studios or shops to house your tools and have a place to practice your skill. One of my city-dwelling aunts goes to a studio where she can set up a loom for her weaving. Look for classes that interest you at your farmers' market, extension office, parks and rec, community colleges, and, of course, the Internet.

No homestead appears overnight. Focus on one skill or hobby at a time. Share that skill with others and learn from them. If your apartment complex or neighborhood coordinates, one neighbor might grow enough apples for the entire neighborhood while another produces a year's worth of salsa. Fun and useful!

Feeding the Family

With the ram pump operating, we needed a way to store the delivered water in our garden. We also wanted a system to store a large volume of water in the event of wildfire, a dreadfully real occurrence where we live. Because of our limited budget, we are resourceful at using things on hand or that we can obtain free or inexpensively. We located a 300-gallon food grade plastic container on Craigslist. It had been purchased new by three young men attending Burning Man festivities in the California desert, who wisely brought a large amount of water with them. Opportunely, they sought to off-load the tank at the same time we hunted for one.

In our attempt to use as little electricity as possible, we planned to use gravity to deliver the ram pump water from the 300-gallon container through the irrigation system. Even though we use a drip system and mulch around our plants to use as little water as possible, electric bills add up when we irrigate straight from the well. In order to use gravity instead, we had to store our water higher than the garden. We had some old galvanized pallet racking sitting on the ground that we had bought years before at a hardware surplus store. We set it up along the

Water tower
at edge of garden

outbuilding that forms one of the walls of our garden. Its height is over 20 feet tall, with the platform for the water tank at about 15 feet. We took apart some of the stalls in the barn to retrieve enough wood to build a strong enough platform for over 2,400 pounds. A gallon of water weighs eight pounds plus the weight of the container. Eventually we rolled the tank up an extension ladder in a hazardous and haphazard manner. It landed unscathed on the platform.

Working on our garden and greenhouse areas

Cody then secured the pallet racking to the side and roof of the outbuilding in the event an earthquake or some other event might cause the racking to shift. Our aim was to keep the water and container from ever coming down. Holes were drilled for the hoses. Cody used his plumbing skills to direct water in and out of the container and deal with any overflow water. He also had to deal with directing water to distinct areas of the garden and orchard, depending on water usage. He later modified the system so we can fill the tank from the well when water is insufficient from the ram pump. We can also bypass the tank to water the garden and orchard directly. Jack, as he frequently does, saw both physics and mathematics in action. Homeschooling at its finest!

We suffered holes in the piping to the tank and a surprise freeze, which damaged a valve on the container, but otherwise the ram pump adequately fills the tank. The water tank irrigates exactly as we had hoped. Hooray for old technology.

Fruits and Nuts

In the past, former owners had dry-wheat farmed and grazed animals on our property. The variety and length of fencing they erected for those purposes was astonishing. Much of it was no longer upright, lying helter-skelter, barbed wire tangled and hidden in grass. Although a slight exaggeration, we could not walk ten feet without encountering a fence to walk around. We could not even walk from the driveway into the yard or to the front steps because there was a tiny fence, with no gate. Needless to say, we took down miles and miles of fencing. Only one fenced area was erected "properly," as Cody would say as he took out his level. In that half-acre area sits the original homesteader barn and our orchard.

We planted grapes and pear, apple, peach, plum, and walnut trees. Friends who are also embarking on a homesteading experience are particularly interested in apple trees. They showed us how to graft, resulting in success with those trees. Because of their diminutive size, we purchased a few larger trees to obtain big crops sooner. Additionally, a scattering of a dozen old apple trees grace the landscape, thriving with much pruning and mulching.

We grew enough apples to press a little cider, but produced an insufficient amount for winter storage. Last year, we attended a homesteading fair where collectors showed their steam engines, sharing more knowledge than an encyclopedia and finding a willing audience in Cody. Cody hit it off with one man in particular, exchanging contact information. Later, the man called us to bring our cider press to one of his pressing parties. Generously, he offered to give us apples, asking how many boxes we could use. Cody said "how about two." Upon arriving at the man's orchard, Cody learned a box meant 900 pounds of apples. Remember, he requested two. He had to lay down the tailgate of his truck in order to fit in both boxes. The truck strained as it was grossly overweight. Cody drove home with a mixture of elation for all of the apples and fear of a broken axle. We ate some, pressed some into cider, dried some, and made apples into pies and sauce. To alleviate the apple problem, we arranged several pressing parties to put a more substantial dent in the quantity.

For the parties, we wanted to move the apples from the shop to the side yard. Because the apples weighed so much, the only way to unload them or move them involved use of our 50-year old forklift, dubbed the "pavement queen." Why? She is clearly not intended for off-concrete use. After investigation, Cody determined the yard to be hard enough to take the queen out for a spin. Everything was going well, and the first box was unloaded. As he moved the second box, bringing it through the front yard he found the soft spot. The queen was mired. We tolerated her as yard art for the next week. Pleasing to the eye, she was not. A week later, the ground froze, and with the help of physics, a winch, and much consternation, the queen was dislodged. Forever banished to her realm in the shop.

Fresh from our garden

Our finished
greenhouse
and apple-crate
raised-bed planters

Garden

We homestead in an alpine-forested area where we must protect our
garden from deer, elk, and rabbits. We settled on an area close to the
house, practically free from shade trees, and began construction of an
eight-foot high perimeter fence. Deer are fierce here. Anything shorter
is inadequate. We reused fence posts from those we had dug out around
the homestead. A retired neighbor stopped to give us a hand, shocked
that we planned to align the posts and fence perfectly with the building,
which abuts one side. I admit to thinking that Cody was a bit obsessive
when insisting we put everything in perfectly level and square, but I
appreciate the results now. We did not have money for a tall gate, so we
welded together some weather-beaten gates left by previous owners. Our
irrigation system consists of mostly secondhand pipe, too.

We quickly found we also needed to protect our garden from bold
gophers. Jack and I sat under one of our maple trees one day as a hearty,
well-fed gopher popped out of his hole and announced his presence
to us. Speaking to neighbors, we realized planting directly in the
ground was essentially providing a giant salad bar for the local gopher

population. Our gardening was growing more complicated than we had anticipated. Based on recommendations, we decided to put in 4 x 4 raised bed boxes with wire mesh in the bottom. The size of the boxes was determined based upon some serious calculations: the boxes were free! Well-worn wooden orchard bins were being retired for plastic ones. However, we did gamble and put pumpkins, squash, and zucchinis directly in the ground. Yes, plants disappeared overnight. Argh, gophers!

The first year, we put in eight boxes for a total of 128 square feet of "protected" gardening. Then we added 16 more boxes. Currently we have 36 4 x 4 garden boxes, containing mostly vegetables and flowers. Cody calls that my side, and his side of the garden contains the 75-foot rows of blueberries and raspberries. We purchased red raspberries and transplanted wild black raspberries from our forest. They seem to have adjusted well to their more cultivated status. By claiming sides, Cody perpetuates a theory Jack articulated when he was almost three. I told Jack his diet had been poor of late, too many cookies, candy, bread, and hot dogs, and I intended to feed him more fruits and vegetables. He told me, "Vegetables and fruits are lady food, and eggs and nuts are man food. That's what Pappa and Granddad eat." While Cody and Jack love the majority of fruits, they also consume plenty of vegetables. I pride myself on being an expert food hider, including vegetables, beans, and other nutritious herbs and food they refuse to eat.

Jack and I constantly engage in two battles in the garden and it appears he has hereto won both. First, he finds rabbits to be cute, while I only find rabbits cute when they have not infiltrated my garden. I now plant a

Putting up fencing and berry trellis

little extra and hope they go for the zucchinis. I neither admit nor deny occasionally letting the dogs out to keep the rabbits looking for greener pastures elsewhere. The second battle involves Jack's attempts to dig a hole to China — in the garden. He can head out in the morning and a few hours later I find a 3 foot by 3 foot by 3 foot hole beside a blueberry bush. His industriousness impresses me, but I would love to allocate such energy away from established plant roots and toward where I need a hole dug! I sense his pain as he says, "Mamma, I spent hours digging this and now you are going to make me fill it in?" "Yes." We have since relegated him to one area of the garden, and he literally pushes those limits. Despite the six-foot buffer we firmly established between his area and some bushes, I can barely squeeze by with my wheelbarrow without tumbling into a deep pit. Somehow, I endure. I like his company more than I mind his testing of the boundaries.

Some orchard boxes were received in deplorable shape. They function as compost bins. Some people enjoy going to the beach, others to a baseball game, and I like adding to and turning my compost (okay, I like the beach too). Cody has made composting gifts for me: forging a sturdy rake for turning and constructing a screen to filter finished compost. I love that food scraps and plants transform into a material beneficial for growing more fruit and vegetables. Composting is simply a mixture of leaves, food scraps, grass clippings, plant matter, and manure piled together and allowed to decay. The smaller the material, the faster it decomposes. A number of friends push compost material through wood chippers to speed the process. The pile should be an approximate mixture of 1 part nitrogen to 25 parts carbon. Nitrogen is found in manure, hay, grass clippings, food waste, seaweed, and coffee, while carbon is found in wood ashes, corn stalks, sawdust, straw, shredded newspaper and cardboard, pine needles, and wood chips. A slight odor usually indicates an excess of nitrogen, which means decomposition is happening. You can add dry leaves, paper, or cardboard to alleviate the smell a bit. Too much carbon slows decomposition too much, so add material high in nitrogen.

Ideally, your pile should be at least 3 feet x 3 feet x 3 feet. The more you turn the pile, the more quickly it decomposes. Turning it also keeps it from becoming a slimy, stinky mess, and keeps air in your pile, necessary for the microbes breaking down the pile. My bins are slatted, which allows air to enter from the bottom of the pile. You can also add bulky material to the bottom to provide adequate aeration of the pile.

You want to keep the pile damp, about as moist as a wrung-out sponge, to keep the decomposing bacteria alive. Compost piles heat up, in part based on size, and in part based on materials. If on the cool side, weed seeds will not be killed so you might not want to add them. If the pile really heats up, it can actually catch fire. This is rare, but keep this in mind when locating your pile. I once caught my pile on fire due to embers left in the

Preparing to work in our compost bins

wood ashes I had recently added. Not the same, but exciting nonetheless. The compost pile can easily halve in size as it "cooks" down. Red worms help your pile decompose quickly, but earthworms help to a lesser extent and arrive as soon as the piling begins. Avoid adding meat, grease, and fat or rodents will be attracted to the pile.

A few helpful hints. Leaves usually take a long time to decompose. I have six composting bins. Two are for long-term decomposition and include bulky material (sunflower stalks, entire bushes) and leaves. I keep them separate because I know they will not be ready in weeks, but rather in months, but they are worth composting because of the fantastic material they produce. Fresh manure can burn plant roots, so you want to make certain it has decomposed adequately. Used sparingly it can really heat up a slow compost pile. You can also add a bit of active compost to get a new pile started. Some people put their fall compost directly on their garden beds. This avoids moving the compost from one location to the next. Just be careful the heat from the pile does not kill any perennial plants or, conversely, inadvertently seed a garden bed with weeds or unwanted plants. This type of composting can also attract extra slugs.

One year we built a cold frame greenhouse so I could start plants sooner in the spring. We again scrounged around to come up with the bulk of the materials. We had no animals, so we took apart the stalls in the barn for interior wood. The barn doors had been hung improperly by previous owners and had fallen off one winter. We took the doors apart, cut them to length, and used them to side the greenhouse. The greenhouse serves as a retreat on cold spring days, promising a warmer future. We live in zone three, based on the USDA Plant Hardiness Zone Map, based on the average annual minimum winter temperature, and the standard to determine which plants thrive at various locations. Twenty minutes from us, at a lower elevation, friends garden at zone seven. This means I put out my tomato plants on the 4th of July, while my friends put them out in late May. Because of our elevation and short growing season, I grow tomatoes and peppers in the greenhouse in the summer. I also experiment with putting them outside. Results are mixed. I guess if my salsa and chutneys last until I can make more from vegetables I grow, results would be defined as adequate.

Because the greenhouse is unheated, I start most of my plants in our dining room. This is a yearly occurrence, so we painted shelves to match the color of trim around the window so the months of seeds in trays and small starts do not overwhelm our attempts to remain civilized. Once the

Showing the variety of plants in our garden and Jack's treehouse nearby

weather warms enough, the starts are brought to the greenhouse, until all danger of frost occurs. Last year, June 14 was our last unofficial frost date.

Wild Edibles

Inevitably, while walking through the garden, someone points to the dandelion and sorrel, suggesting we eat it. It is funny to be foraging directly in the garden path, but they are nutritious. In the forest, we find wild black raspberries, alpine strawberries, huckleberries, and blackberries, although our favorite food to forage is mushroom. While we have made minimal attempts at cultivating mushrooms, and failed, we love foraging for them. In the Pacific Northwest, mushrooms grow prodigiously well in the damp, mossy conditions. Chanterelles are our go-to. Jack is the spotter; he has eagle eyes. Cody loves to hunt for them under bushes and ferns. While I like hiking around and poking in a glorious forest, I mainly appreciate the garlic and butter accompanying the mushrooms later. At first, we feared we would grab poisonous look-a-likes by accident. Our former neighbors feared too. We received an email from one thanking us for the bag of chanterelles we had left at their door. They tasted divine and were eaten in great quantities. The email had been posted shortly after eating as they were afraid they might not be around long enough to thank us.

Jack has learned chanterelles offer a business opportunity. On one excursion, Cody told Jack he could sell all of the mushrooms we found. Never before has Jack enjoyed mushroom hunting so much, or wanted to stay out long after Cody and I were ready to leave. I cleaned so many mushrooms in which I was unable to partake. The horror! Early the following morning, I drove Jack into town for errands and mushroom selling. He had been discussing the price at which he

was willing to sell them. We arrived at one of the local markets and he asked me to carry the mushrooms in for him, weighing too much for an eight-year-old to carry comfortably. I cannot recall the exact figures, but Jack looks to be a shrewd businessman. I said not a word as he negotiated telling the owner he had calculated being paid more than was being offered. A deal was struck. Proud mamma. Plus, Jack bought dessert for the family the next time we ate out.

Young Cody and his catch of the day

Fishing

As a teenager, Cody walked to the river every day, catching salmon and steelhead when in season. He traveled several miles to fish, both before and after school, keeping his fishing pole in his locker. He built lures, tied flies, and crafted custom fishing rods, selling them to friends and people who heard about them by word of mouth. This persisted until he turned 20 or so and moved to the city. Now back in the countryside, his previous obsession is reemerging. We have fished for salmon and halibut in the recent past, and last year Cody and Jack camped and fished with friends. The ocean and many rivers in the area provide ample cod, halibut, and salmon. While not a regular habit, the small investment of a pole and license make fishing an affordable and delicious day outside.

Hunting

Growing up, hunting was the vacation for families in Cody's church. Hunting camps included multiple families, up to one hundred people in each camp. Canvas wall tents were erected with stoves inside. The camp was run like a military mission. They meant business. There was a harvest to gather. They hunted the same location for decades, knowing where animals bedded and holed up. They hunted in drives, with children beating bushes to push the animals to sharpshooters at the other end of the clearing.

While for some it was purely pleasure, for others the meat would feed the family for the rest of the year. Elk provides an enormous quantity of

Cody and a photo of his granddad
who taught him numerous skills

meat, comparable to a cow. Back then, you averaged one elk every seven
years, so people relied upon each other to up the average. Packing the
meat and antlers out of places like Idaho and Oregon's Hells Canyon
proved so difficult that an entire day was spent to carry a pack of 50 to 55
pounds. The boys packed meat for the older men. When you were older,
the younger would pack your meat. It was a rite of passage.

Cody's granddad started hunting in 1946 and never missed a season,
hunting well into his 80s. Cody loved his maternal granddad greatly
and spent an inordinate amount of time with him. Before Cody was old
enough to take the hunter safety course, he was "devastated" for the four
weeks Granddad left to shoot elk and deer. Most men took two weeks'
vacation for elk hunting and another two for deer hunting, which was
warmer, so the women came along.

The first year of hunting came with great anticipation. Cody left his
parents at home, heading out alone with his granddad. Cody's dad gave
him his paternal granddad's rifle, a vintage WWII Mauser eight-milli-
meter rifle. Because of its weight, and Cody's slight size, they cut three
inches off the stock so he could fire it. Cody's parents, concerned he
would be cold, put him in warm, nylon ski clothes, unlike his granddad,
who always wore wool everything. For his feet, they bought moon boots.

Unfortunately, and not unexpectedly, Cody and his granddad neither saw nor shot any animals. As hunters might surmise, Cody was the biggest deterrent to the hunt. Nylon and moon boots create a tremendous amount of noise, much like wearing a bell around the neck. Granddad never said a word. He led Cody around on an "exciting," long, two-week hunt, even though he knew they would never see anything. The next season he personally took Cody to the store, taking charge of buying his wool hunting clothes. That year's hunting was much quieter, and successful.

Cody and his granddad hunted deep in the canyons, the best hunting in the bottom. Cody's granddad outfitted them in lightweight backpacking equipment, hiking down the night before hunting season started, camping halfway down to watch deer and elk. They went to sleep only "a gunshot away" from the animals. Others took hours to scramble down into the canyon, while Cody and his granddad could hunt alone, at length, before others arrived. Competition was fierce for animals. Elk and deer scatter after they hear the first shots. The element of surprise is important.

As a teenager, Cody lay in a prone position, resting his rifle over a log, and squeezed the trigger on a nice large four-point buck across the canyon. With a single shot, you cannot locate the direction of the shot from the sound. A hunter fires a second shot to identify the location (ranging it). He heard a stick break, a snap, and looked over his shoulder to see who in his hunting party approached. In reality, with only a single shot fired, a bear spooked, and emerged from its resting spot. Cody lay downwind of it, roughly 40 feet. Quickly he flipped over on his back and rested his rifle on his knees. He peered through the scope as the bear approached. As he looked through the riflescope, he only saw green and

brown. To his horror, the magnification was on nine, reserved for shots over several hundred yards. He panned to the left until he saw green, and stopped. Then back again. Back and forth. Green. Brown. Green. He stopped at brown and pulled the trigger.

He felt excited. He felt terrified. The bear failed to drop. Cody waited, still on his back, the bear now only 20 feet away — some of the slowest moments of his life. Finally, it ran back into the woods. Dreadfully foolish, Cody ran in after it. It growled the most frightening, horrible roar. Cody turned around and ran for 15 minutes, until he could breathe no more. A few hours later, after giving it ample time to succumb, Cody returned. The bear weighed all of 350 pounds, forcing it to be butchered in place — a nasty, greasy job, like grabbing a bar of soap, but knowing it is not. Cody found he could barely hold onto his knife. His adrenaline was used up. He was tired. He still had to carry the bear out. The buck too. He gave the bear to someone in camp who had a taste for bear. He is not a fan.

A vastly different skill and season, Cody also bow-hunted. Rules and tactics differ from conventional hunting. Cody recalls his hunting stories with great fondness, deeming himself fortunate to have participated in the ritual aspect of it, the anticipation of the young boys so wanting to go, and getting the first hunting license and rifle. This was a step from childhood into manhood. It is something we plan to introduce to Jack when he is old enough. For now, we admit to enjoying our neighbor's grass-fed beef, butchered for us. Fortunately, Cody knows how to butcher when the time comes. Some skills are never forgotten.

https://goo.gl/lbKN7n

The Larder:
Preserving Food, Preserving Life

Where do you store all of these tasty morsels, you might wonder? The kitchen housed a closet/kitchen pantry combination we converted into a pantry only. We took out the hooks and clothing rod and added additional shelving. Because the kitchen contains few cabinets, this essentially tripled my storage space. A dirt basement lies under a small section of the house. Much of it is crawl space, but there exists a concrete pad measuring roughly 8" x 15". The pad currently accommodates washer and dryer, water pressurizer, water filter, and the hot water heater. We plan to move the washer and dryer from there to another location in the house. At that time, we intend to line the edges of the concrete with shelves to form a pantry/root cellar. Currently, the heat and humidity from the appliances create an inconsistent environment, so we are unable to store fruit or root vegetables for an extended time. However, we started a pantry there by constructing one wall of shelves. The farmhouse was originally a log cabin built in 1903. Numerous additions have taken place, including a second story. We decided to put the wall directly under one of the beams to reinforce the foundation.

Putting up or putting by are two common terms to describe how to preserve the food you harvested, foraged, butchered, and caught. At mealtimes, I frequently point to ingredients in the food and say, "That is from my garden," or "I canned the berries we picked," or "Remember when we found those in the forest?" Preserved food is a source of satisfaction and security. A few years ago, I enrolled in a Master Food Preservers program put on by the state extension office. It is akin to Master Gardeners, where you learn an inordinate amount and then realize how little you really know. I feel more secure in my food preservation, but less willing to eat goodies from those who may not adhere to standard safety techniques. Strangely enough, I have never genuinely enjoyed food poisoning. Successful completion of the course does not mean I am a "master" or expert in food preservation, but it does mean I gained education and experience. I now help with food safety and technique classes offered in the area, as well as volunteer at farmers' markets and the like. I find I possess more creativity in the kitchen because I know how to play within safe food parameters.

Below are some methods to preserve food you harvest, forage, or purchase. This is only an overview and you will want more detailed information before getting started.

Freezing

Freezing is the least time-consuming food preservation method. I use it most regularly when we over-pick (160 pounds of blueberries in one day), overbuy (monthly trip to Costco), overharvest (zucchinis), or overcook (leftovers).

In addition to my kitchen freezer, we also rely on an upright freezer we purchased new. We gambled with two used freezers in the past and lost both times. We decided on a small upright for a few reasons. First, when I had a large chest freezer, I never knew what was buried in the bottom. I also found it difficult to find the necessary food, and when I did, retrieving it required taking out a dozen bags or boxes while performing gymnastics to reach the outermost corners of the freezer. Then I would toss the dozen frozen items back into the abyss and further add to the disorganized chaos. I realize chest freezers work for some, but not for me. In the upright, I can see what food remains and keep the freezer more orderly. I purposefully bought a small size for that reason. It takes less room, so I can place it close to the kitchen, whereas my chest freezer was located in an outbuilding. Thus, we actually use the food that is in it.

Authors dedicate entire books to freezing, so I will not attempt to outline everything, but I have listed a few of my favorite tips below.

- Close your freezer properly. We have a key and lock on our freezer. When it is near bursting, you need to ensure it is properly shut. It is disheartening to find a freezer in the basement or garage with the door ajar and hundreds of dollars of food ruined. Ask my parents. Oops. Sorry. Some friends of ours installed an alarm sounding when the freezer stays open too long. Annoying when you are rummaging around in it, but a lifesaver otherwise.

- Cool all foods and liquids before putting them in the freezer. Hot foods melt cold food and can ruin the taste and texture of the food already in the freezer.

- Leave room for expansion and remove as much air as possible. Liquids, even within food, expand. Blueberries can burst bags. Soups can shatter glass. An experienced voice here!

- Avoid clumping. When freezing berries, tomatoes, or pieces of food, freeze them on a cookie sheet and then transfer them to a plastic bag.

- Blanch vegetables properly. Under-blanching stimulates enzyme activity. Over-blanching results in a cooked product and loss of flavor, color, and nutrients.

- Use ice cube trays to make small portions of sauces, broths, stock, and pesto. Easy to grab them out of a plastic bag while cooking.

Fermenting

Most food preservation is a science, done with exactitude, or quality and safety can be diminished. Fermenting is the creative side of preservation — an art, where you can take numerous liberties. It ranges from sauerkraut, pickles, sourdough bread, cheese, kefir, vinegar, soy sauce, and miso to yogurt. Unlike most types of preservation, incredibly, fermentation actually increases vitamins, probiotics, and minerals and makes them more available for absorption. The fermenting process transforms food into a more digestible food through a chemical alteration. You often see food bubbling as it ferments. To stop fermentation, simply put the food in a cool place or refrigerator.

My everyday fermenting includes yogurt, sourdough, and sauerkraut. With yogurt and sourdough, I use a starter. For yogurt, I usually take plain yogurt I purchase at the store, add milk, and heat it to 185°F. This prepares the milk proteins for yogurt culture production. Too hot and it kills probiotics. I then pour the combination into glass containers and keep it warm for approximately eight hours. That is it. Yogurt done. Flavor to taste.

No-knead bread in front of homemade scrap wall

More exciting is sourdough bread. A sourdough starter is both the homesteader's and artisan baker's best friend, a mixture of wild yeast and bacteria living in flour and water. Regular baker's yeast is an entirely distinct ingredient. Because a starter is living, you must feed it regularly or it dies. When you prepare to bake, or make pancakes, you take half of the starter for your food and feed the other half. It grows at room temperature, allowing you to take more when you next desire some. Put the starter in the refrigerator to stop growth and preserve it. Either cultivate your own starter, literally capturing wild yeast for baking, or obtain a known starter, admittedly the easier method.

I received my starter from a friend whose uncle purchased it over 30 years ago. The story goes that a Forest Service employee in Idaho created truly delicious sourdough breads and biscuits. Despite pestering, he refused to share his sourdough starter. Finally, he indulged the local community by donating a sample to a fundraiser auction. My friend's uncle won the bid, and also became known for his extraordinary sourdough delights. When my friend graduated high school, he received some starter as a gift from his uncle. Ultimately, this helped to influence him to attend culinary school. When I met him, he worked as a professional baker who used the starter at his place of employment. In full disclosure, I forgot to feed the first starter I received from him and killed it. Regardless of my shame, I confessed my dereliction of duty and requested a second attempt at the Forest Service starter. It lives! I have shared this starter, too. It definitely is the gift that keeps giving and giving. Exceptionally interesting that food we eat daily contains an ingredient over 30 years old! No expiration date here.

Other fermentation does not necessitate a starter, but rather uses a brine or salt over an ingredient. To make plain sauerkraut, I mix salt and cabbage and press to expel water from the vegetable, thereby creating its own brine. I then place a plate or something to weigh the cabbage down, allowing no air to reach the cabbage, and wait for the magic to happen. That is it. You can add all kinds of vegetables for color and taste. At room temperature, the cabbage begins to ferment. I leave it there until it is ready. "Ready" simply means it reaches a taste I like. The length of time varies from three or four days in the summer to weeks in the winter. Once I put my finished product in the refrigerator, it stops the fermenting process, where it keeps for months. Yes, recipes differ. There are many ways to skin the proverbial cat (and make sauerkraut).

Fermenting is exciting. Do not be afraid to try it. Worst-case scenario, you are out a few dollars. Best-case scenario, you create a nutritious, delicious delicacy in which to indulge.

Cody's sister helps pit cherries from our orchard.

Canning/Pressure Canning

Canning is the correct time for your inner "safety Sally" to appear. I have heard and read stories of canning that would make your hair stand on end. "No one has died yet" is a poor standard for food safety. Open-kettle canning, steam canners, and processing in conventional ovens, microwave ovens, and dishwashers is not recommended. Processing is inconsistent, and seals appear tight when they may not be. Spoilage can occur and health is at risk.

There are only two reliable, prudent methods of canning food at home — boiling water bath canning and pressure canning. Generally, high-acid foods like fruits, pickles, jams, and jellies can be safely processed in a boiling water bath, where the temperature reaches 212°F. Acids, such as vinegar, lemon, and lime juice can be added to some low-acid foods, allowing them to be canned in a boiling water bath. Common examples include pickles, tomatoes, chutneys, and some salsas. Low-acid foods,

including meat, vegetables, and seafood, require processing in a pressure canner, where the temperature can reach 240°F or higher, which can only be achieved under pressure. This pressure is achieved by trapping steam in the pressure canner. Pressure canning is not the same as pressure cooking and uses different equipment!

Bacteria and spores in low-acid foods can survive the temperature of boiling water. Of greatest concern is Clostridium botulinum, commonly known as botulism, which cannot be detected via smell, taste, or sight, and is potentially fatal. While it is usually found in improperly canned vegetables and fish, it has been detected in tomato-based mixtures and fruits, ranging from mangoes to peaches to pears to applesauce. Apparently, high-acid foods improperly processed can permit growth of bacteria, molds, or yeasts that can change the pH of the food, allowing the growth of Clostridium botulinum. This is not meant to scare you, only to highly suggest you follow recently tested recipes.

Cody's great grandmother's canner, restored

Reliable resources include The National Center for Home Food Preservation website (http://nchfp.uga.edu/) and the following books: the *USDA Complete Guide to Home Canning, So Easy to Preserve,* or the *Ball Blue Book.* All contain research-based recipes. Unfortunately, out-of-date recipes often fail to take into account essential criteria regarding altitude adjustment, canning methods with high failure rates, and the pH change of many of our fruits and vegetables. The majority of people forget that the temperature of boiling water decreases as altitude increases. Thus, when pressure canning, pressure must be increased half a pound for every 1,000 feet of elevation. Without making the correct changes, the food is under-processed, and has an increased risk of botulism. Adjustments in processing time must be made when water bath canning as well.

To highlight the need for up-to-date and tested recipes, take tomatoes for example. Previously, it was thought safe to process them via boiling water bath. However, the pH in the heirloom and conventional tomatoes can vary dramatically. You cannot tell the pH by looking at them, knowing the seed source, or testing them at home. If you purchase low-acid tomatoes from the grocery or farmers' market and overlook adding an acid, there is potential for food poisoning. While you may be healthy and able to weather an illness, if you give the canned tomatoes to an elderly person or diabetic, you could be passing along hardship or even death. Additionally, tested recipes give tips like (1) green tomatoes are more acidic than ripened tomatoes, (2) tomatoes from dead or frost-killed vines cannot be canned — freeze them instead, and (3) use of a pressure canner with tomatoes results in more nutritious canned tomato products.

After proper canning is complete, jars should be kept in cool, dark places. While the food should remain safe to eat, check it. When in doubt, throw it out. Eat the oldest food first. Food not sauced or pureed usually deteriorates in quality — green beans, peaches, and pickles lose firmness. When canning season starts, I carry the bulk of the last year's jars from the basement to my kitchen pantry, so we eat those jars first. All new jars go to the basement. In fact, I canned so much from last year's harvest, I have not unpacked all of my jars from the boxes used to carry them to the basement. A friend gave me heaps of plums resulting in Chinese plum sauce, plum chutney, plum jam, and blueberry plum jam. Not the worst problem to have.

Dehydration

Food dehydration has occurred as long as there has been sun. Today, you can dry foods via various methods, including solar, vine drying, oven, and dehydrators. Fruits, herbs, vegetables, fruit leather, and meat can be dehydrated, along with some foods many people overlook. Dehydrated foods last longer, take up less storage room, and weigh less. They fit well in emergency kits or when backpacking. One friend backpacked for months and dehydrated her own food rather than buy freeze-dried, saving money and, likely, her health. Her stash included dehydrated tomato sauce for pasta, dehydrated beans for burritos, dehydrated fruit for snacking, and lots of dehydrated vegetables to add to various meals.

No matter what you decide to dehydrate, make certain the food is the same size; varying thicknesses means varying drying times. You can

Dehydrated peaches

rehydrate many types of food. Think about instant potatoes or oatmeal! Someone dehydrated them for you. Add reconstituted ingredients to soups, casseroles, and pies. Powders rehydrate to roughly a quarter of their fresh state and most fruit and vegetables to one-half.

Solar dehydration is the simplest method because it requires no appliances. The best-known examples are raisins dried from grapes. The high acidity and sugar content of fruit makes them safe for solar dehydration. Vegetables and meats are not recommended for solar drying. Meats are high in protein, making them more sensitive to microbial growth. Vegetables lack enough sugar and acid. Warm temperatures, low humidity, and a constant breeze provide the best conditions for drying fruit outdoors. Humidity under 60 percent and temperatures above 85°F are best. Depending on your conditions, you should bring fruit indoors overnight. As temperatures lower at night, relative humidity increases, causing condensation (dew), which adds moisture back to your fruit if left outdoors. This not only slows the drying process but increases spoilage concerns. When setting fruit in the sun, put it on a non-reactive surface, as some metals react with the high acid content of fruit. Preferable are screens or racks you can raise up to allow air circulation around the food. Place a screen or rack both under and on top to protect fruit from birds, animals, insects, and debris. Cheesecloth or some type of netting work too.

You can also buy a solar box or use your car. Really. Imagine how hot your car becomes on a summer day. See — you already bought a solar dehydrator! Crack the windows of your car to allow air circulation. Place the trays in the back window ledge or wherever the sun strikes most.

Vine drying is the other method of drying out-of-doors. Beans are a common example of vine drying. Leave the beans (navy, kidney, butter, great northern, lima, lentils, and soybeans) in their pods on the vine until the beans inside rattle. When the vines and pods dry and shrivel, pick the beans and shell them. No pretreatment is necessary. If beans are still moist, the drying process is not complete and the beans will mold if not more thoroughly dried. If needed, drying can be completed in the sun, oven, or a dehydrator.

Others examples consist of sunflower seeds and sturdy herbs. With sunflowers, the heads should be cut off, leaving a stem of roughly a foot. Tie a cloth bag around the head to catch any seeds that might fall out.

Hang upside-down in a dry location with good air movement. Sturdy herbs such as thyme, rosemary, sage, and parsley can be tied into tiny bundles and air-dried.

Sundried fruits and vine-dried items should be pasteurized to kill any insects and eggs. Pasteurization is simple. Place in an oven at 160°F for 30 minutes. Or seal the food in a freezer-safe plastic bag, and place in a freezer set at 0°F or less for 48 hours. Then condition any fruit and store.

All dehydrated fruit should be conditioned. Conditioning distributes excess moisture from fruit piece to piece, reducing the chance of spoilage. Loosely pack the dried fruit pieces in plastic or glass containers and cover them with plastic wrap and then the container's lid. Shake them daily for approximately four days. The drier pieces absorb moisture from the other pieces. If you notice moisture in the container, you want to dehydrate all of the pieces a bit more.

More modern methods of dehydrating include dehydrators or ovens. Microwaves are fabulous for herbs, retaining taste and color, but are not good for other foods. A food dehydrator is a small electrical appliance with an electric heat element, generally operating at 140°F. Vents and a fan provide air circulation. Assorted styles and accessories allow for special racks and higher volumes.

Ovens dry more slowly than food dehydrators because they lack fans for air circulation. You can crack the door and set a fan by the oven door to create air movement. Without a fan, it ordinarily takes twice as long to dry food in an oven. It also takes more electricity than a food dehydrator.

Finally — store the food. Store the dehydrated food in a moisture resistant, airtight container. Glass, plastic, and non-galvanized metal are normally your best choices. Then place the container out of sunlight and excess heat.

Homeschooling in the garden — it's not Robin Hood — it's Rhubarb Hood.

Timber Framing (Part 1)

When discussing timber framing, it can include any step in the process from felling a tree (or using a windfall) to trimming the log, milling your own lumber, or the precision work of joinery — making joints that hold without glue or nails. Tools are the focus of this "how to."

Any project like this begins with talking about tools. You will need a basic set. It doesn't require much and I don't have the best — there are faster and fancier things, but what I have works. It's a good solid set that gets the job done at a minimal price.

Tools and Timbers

STANDARD METAL SQUARE: Everything starts with the layout, and the 1.5 inch by 2 inch square was made for timber framing. These are the widths of the mortices. You will lay it along the edge of the board to square the edges.

TAPE MEASURE: The only other measuring tool you will need is a tape measure, but when it comes to timber framing, precision is very important. One 25- or 30-foot measure would be fine. It needs to be one that is easy to read, and measurements in the 32nds are best. It takes the guesswork out of things.

STEEL RULER *(optional)*: A steel ruler is also nice for layout because you get more precision without the unwanted flexing of a tape measure. It's nice to have but not necessary.

COMBINATION *(optional -speed square or a squangle)*: You can use these to figure the angles, for example for rafters if you are building a cabin project. You can use a speed square for a lot of things too, including holding it down firmly as a rip guide or fence to get a straight cut with a skill saw. That is a carpenter's secret. The smaller combination squares are nice for measuring depth.

CARPENTER'S HATCHET *(optional)*: They are beveled like a chisel. It is designed for precise control with a finger notch and wider beard (lower edge of ax blade) and the poll (flat back of the ax head) can be used to hammer nails. Some have notches to pull nails.

1.5 INCH CHISEL: Timber framing chisels are the bread and butter of the whole process. This is the place you need to spend your money. These will be your most valuable and treasured items, and the things you take the most care of. Three chisels

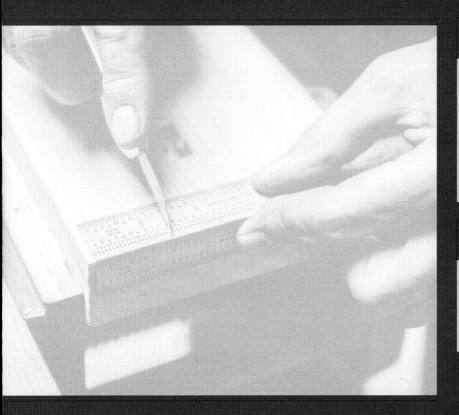

are typically used in timber framing. The first one I would buy is the 1.5-inch chisel. A lot of the vintage chisels are nice, but quality chisels are being produced and sold today. These need to be some of your sharpest tools.

3.0 TO 3.5-INCH SLICK: My second purchase would be a slick, a very large chisel. It is used for flattening out tenons and lots of other things. It is basically a plane. Mine is a vintage slick that was made in 1837, a beautiful one made of forge-welded, laminated steel. It's a beautiful tool and a real treasure for me. These need to be incredibly sharp.

2.0-INCH CHISEL: This would be my third purchase. Good chisels will have a metal ring at the end of the handle. When you strike them with a tool, using a wood or poly mallet, the wood in the handle will not mushroom because the metal ring protects it. I have beat on these chisels a long time and there is no issue. You just do not want to strike them with a metal hammer.

WOODEN OR POLY MALLET: Some people like to be purists and use the wood. I have used both and prefer the poly. When I am doing detail work and watching the chisel end carefully, if I get tired or lazy and don't hit the chisel square on the end, it tends not to glance off and hit my hand. It's just a little bit rubbery or sticky.

HEAVY DUTY DRILL: You will want a good, really strong heavy-duty drill with a half-inch chuck for drilling holes into or through the timbers. (You can use a cordless drill for some aspects of timber framing, such as drilling a series of holes that you can trim out with the chisels for notches.)

AUGER STYLE DRILL BITS: A 1.5-inch bit is all you need until we do our pins and treenails. Mine I got off of Ebay and it was really a great find. The size and heft are so much better than what you can find today. You can re-sharpen them, and if you take care of them, you can use them indefinitely. The auger-style bits pull themselves in and are really great bits.

LONG DRILL BITS: These will correspond to the length and diameter of the treenails you will need. For a one-inch treenail, you will need a one-inch bit. For a half-inch treenail, you need a half-inch drill bit. A treenail (also called a trenail, trennel, or trunnel) is simply a wooden peg or pin, or even dowel, that you use to fasten two pieces of wood together.

CARPENTER'S HANDSAW: One other tool you will want to spend some money on, and take care of or have a vintage one sharpened, is a proper carpenter's saw. A lot of us may have used our dad's, but if you pick it up and try it, it's slow and we grab a skill saw. But you will be amazed how well and efficiently a properly sharpened, tuned, and used carpenter's saw will work. If you look around some, you can still find people who sharpen them. So if you find a well-tapered saw, you can have them restored and sharpened. If you take care of it, this is all you need.

DRAW KNIFE: You can use it to remove defects, bark, or wane in the timber without hurting the structural integrity of the timber. They need to be sharp. Vintage ones are very good, but new ones can be found. You don't see these old types of tools very often.

SKILL SAW: This is the essential tool for anyone. You can use this to easily square the wooden timber edges and other places when needed. With this one tool you can do about anything, even build a house. If I needed to choose one tool to build something, this would be it. This will replace a table saw, a chop saw — it will do everything you need.

If you are going to use it to help with the joinery, it is critical that you square the fence with the saw blade. Just because it reads zero doesn't mean it is. You can loosen the housing and use a speed square to check and adjust as needed (make sure the teeth are not getting in the way). It should be 90 degrees. I recommend you check it every day before you start work. Otherwise, this can give you nightmares.

TO SQUARE THE END OF A TIMBER: Cut each of the four sides of the timber, and then use the carpenter's saw to cut the middle where the saw blade could not reach and the wood is still attached.

TIMBER: Use 4 by 4 or 6 by 6 timbers as needed for your project — either purchased or cut and then milled for yourself. You can also reclaim old timbers for use in new projects. It just takes a little prep work for them to be usable.

To sharpen a chisel

I use the fine side of the stone. Use kerosene or diesel in a bottle as a way to carry away the shavings. Chisels are very easy to sharpen, but you have to keep the stone very straight with the bevel. Move in circles and keep flat to the bevel. Finally, lay the stone on the flat back of the chisel and work away any wirings that may have formed on the edges.

7. Quality Of Life

We endured some difficulties in our move to the country. Circuitous might be one way to describe the route here. Rough, uphill, and jarring might be some others. On our homestead, we still have not "made it." We are making it every day. People imagine a quiet, blissful retreat where we commune with nature and God all day, with no worries. However, we face stress, deadlines, and challenges every day. We purchased a foreclosed property with doors literally falling off the hinges and plumbing leaking through ceilings and walls. We had no extra money to remodel, only to patch the worst. Projects wait to be finished, bills to be paid, schooling to be completed. Yes, the sacrifices we made to acquire our homestead and carve out the life we lead have been worth it. This lifestyle does not cut the workload

Quiet country life

Jack helps out on the homestead.

or the burdens of daily life, but it changes them a bit. No doubt our mountainous, forested setting feeds our soul as much as it pleases our eyes.

As Cody and I reflect on how we got here, we realize a few very important things. We think our lives are quieter and more reflective than if we had remained in the city. The quiet where we live fills your mind differently than urban white noise. We both enjoy manual labor and that feeling of tired satisfaction at the end of the day. Yes, the projects provide ample time to consider all that is right and wrong in our lives and how to make things better, but neither one of us wax poetic while pulling weeds.

Part of the success of this endeavor was due to both of us wanting to create a homestead and be willing to leave our previous home and life. Compromises were made as to location, buildings, career, and what we were willing deal with. However, we each have our unwavering needs and wants; and we respect each other's, even if we do not hold them.

We spend much more time together now than when we lived in the city. We love one another, which is why we married, and genuinely like to be together. We also like Jack, not just as a son but also as a person. God's original plan was for spouses to be helpmates for one another, for the family to work together. In our current culture, families have separate careers, bank accounts, and vacations. While this functions for some families, this type of lifestyle was fracturing our marriage. We needed to be together more, instead of living independently. *"Though one may be overpowered by another, two can withstand him. And a threefold cord is not quickly broken"* (Ecclesiastes 4:12). Certainly, we enjoy our own hobbies and friends. We do our own things and travel separately

Making future plans as a family

occasionally, but not to the extent we did when first married. Not everyone is called to live rurally, homeschool their children, and only work within the confines of the home, but it works for us.

Most women visiting our home claim they could not live "this far out" — they would be lonely and bored. "This far out" was a compromise. One roommate I had found me strange in that I could stay home for days on end without leaving except for time spent in nature. Our whole family is this way, which lends itself to satisfaction living "this far out." Time with friends happens less than previously, and not as spontaneously, with neighbors being a welcome exception. Visits usually extend a bit longer — a full afternoon or day, even overnight, because of the driving commitment. It takes planning to limit our trips into town. Between homeschool co-op, church, errands, activities, and friends, I aim for two visits a week to town, but three often happen. Errands become stacked one after the other, library, bank, grocery store, post office, hardware store, etc. Cody runs my errands and I run his. Texts are sent, "Leaving town soon, anything else?" If we forget something, we do without. Browsing in stores happens infrequently; money is likely saved. While we support our local businesses regularly, some products are not sold here. For those items, the convenience of online ordering cannot be overstated. Deliver to my front porch instead of enduring three or four hours in the car? Yes, please. If we head to town in the morning, little can convince us to return later that same day. Admittedly, it is not that long (depending on your point of view and weather-related road conditions), but it is long enough to turn down invitations and events because of the drive.

I am a bit of an anomaly among my career-oriented friends, in that I chose not to return to my career once Jack was school-aged. While I can miss certain aspects of outside employment, my life, and that of my family, remains better because I stay home. I worked hard to obtain a position of power in a largely male-dominated field. I was often the youngest and one of only a few or the only female in meetings or on a project. I found that the overly assertive quality I needed at my job could be difficult to turn off when I left at the end of the day. While an exceedingly useful trait on occasion, I prefer who I am when I do not need to use it. I paint with a broad brush here, but I have seen when people fight hard to have a successful career, they often carry that fighting mentality to other areas of their lives — even fighting those who love them. Unintentionally, people belittle their mates, always correcting or suggesting better ways to do things. I understand why, but no one wants to be nagged all the time. I am the default organizer and secretary in our marriage and it can be tough. At times I can feel unheard by pressing obligations and projects to be accomplished, and Cody can feel nagged. We realize what causes me stress is not necessarily what causes him stress. It helps us to set up "meetings," discuss it, write lists, and both actively strive to alleviate this issue. We also recognize that we both mess

Every little boy's dream, Jack's beautiful treehouse

up and have some enormous weak spots. We try to extend grace to each other and ourselves.

My mother always wisely said not to have expectations of someone unless you tell them what you want or need beforehand. We simply cannot read each other's minds. Many couples endure disappointment instead of expressing what they really desire. They tear each other down for some imagined slight instead of building each other up. While not perfect, we are a team. We know that we would never hurt each other on purpose, so we give each other the benefit of the doubt. We have each other's back. We would never joke about getting a divorce as some couples do. We chose one another, were blessed in that decision, and will fight to stay together. *"Live joyfully with the wife whom you love all the days of your vain life which He has given you under the sun, all your days of vanity; for that is your portion in life"* (Ecclesiastes 9:9).

We remain a work in progress, but hope we are good role models for Jack in communicating problems kindly and seeking attainable solutions. A friend always says, "We are solution people." I love that. Dwell on the answers and not the problems. Build a strong foundation for a flexible home.

Most importantly — do you know the feeling when you are surrounded by family, friends, and people who love you, but you feel lonely anyway? We are blessed to be able to turn to God then. I was agnostic until I was 30, so understand that not everyone feels this way about God, but for us He is a wonderful comfort and support when things do not go as planned. I lean on Him when I lament choices I make or feel bitter or unloved. If Cody and I experience a rough day, I start to pray and list ways Cody loves me and I love him and his good qualities. Of course, I am quickly overwhelmed by the list and my mood changes completely when I do it. Cody has not changed at all, but my approach to him has. One friend eloquently described our faith as "a strong source of nourishment, support, and inspiration . . . one feeds into the other . . . love of God and from God builds your faith with God . . . to feel and see the same love from Cody builds love in marriage. Cody sees the same, stronger faith, stronger confidence and peace of mind, better team work, positive feedback." We are blessed to have a "sense of peace and support and love" from the Lord and from each other and "confidence grows from it."

Today I work as teacher, secretary, event coordinator, sounding board, and all-around background guru for the Wranglerstar channel, among my many other roles. Apparently, author too. We often joke that I am a Honda Civic and Cody is a Ferrari. We say this because I am pretty easygoing about how life flows — reliable, flexible, and willing to try most anything. Knowing this, if I have a strong desire or opinion, Cody will do almost anything to accommodate me as he realizes it is important to me. Because of this, although difficult to imagine, if the time comes when I wish to seek outside employment, I know Cody will give me his full encouragement and support.

Right now, it feels like Cody's season; that I am to be of support to him. This does not mean a denial of my needs or desires, only that life is sculpting something out of Cody in front of my eyes and I want to see what is emerging. *"And he said to him, 'Son, you are always with me, and all that I have is yours"* (Luke 15:31). I get to share in Cody's joys and successes; I am with him, a marvelous thing. Since moving here, Cody is a changed man. Cody has been able to labor outdoors in the forest and with timber in a way unavailable on our smaller parcels, like an animal uncaged and returned to his rightful habitat. His demeanor has become more peaceful; his eyes flicker with delight more frequently. While some people enjoy nature, Cody belongs in nature, on his knees mucking in the mud, felling timber, climbing trees. His ability to use his hands daily on things he loves has somehow changed how his mind operates. The Bible says your body is the

Cody geared out for a safe climb

Cody conducting
Bible study

temple of God here on earth, and as such, it is important to nourish your body properly, both to honor God and so your mind operates at peak performance. At peak performance, you can best explain why the Lord is worthy of adoration. I think nature feeds Cody's mind so he can better share his love of the Lord and minister to others.

Since Cody met God on the way to the bar, he has always been involved in outreach to others. He used to put pamphlets in each Jeep part box he shipped. Then he began online Bible studies, which he still holds weekly. Living on the homestead, the Lord has allowed Cody, and to a lesser extent me, to share the Lord's love even when we speak of routine daily tasks. I sometimes think we have an accidental ministry. Clearly not an accident on the part of the Lord, but one that was not anticipated. We have agreed to be part of it, despite any reservation or fear we used to hold. When He asks or leads, we look at each other and jump in, most of the time. Sharing the projects we do and life we lead on the homestead has touched many hearts. This may sound corny or overreaching, but we hear from strangers who find strength to do the right thing, who reunite with their families, who have met the Lord through videos on sharpening an ax or getting our truck out of the mud. I would love to say we are so artistic and clever there was no way to avoid acting on our messages of love, family, and integrity, but our video editing is not that good. This ministry has been an enormous part of our move to the homestead, both increasingly demanding and rewarding.

Had we remained in the city or on our small acreage, our lives would have been substantially different. We would not have known each other as well. I think we would have relied upon ourselves more than the Lord. We have experienced our deep need for Him. We find ourselves in the middle of our homesteading experience, certainly not finished in any way. I feel as though we found where we are supposed to be. Our previous homes never felt like they were ours since we kept wanting something else. While we still have unpacked boxes (which I realize we should just donate at this point), this house feels like home. As Jack said shortly after moving here, "I feel like I've lived here my entire life."

Initially, our dream was to work hard at interesting jobs, make good money, buy a nice home, have some children, raise them in the city, and send them to college to do what they wanted to do. Along the way, we discovered our dream should include what we wanted to do. There was nothing wrong with our original dream, but we were not sure it was our dream. As we examined why we continued to feel constantly unsettled, we realized the attributes we were striving for were not particularly important for us. Yes, we still value a fulfilling career, a decent living, etc., but we more deeply desired time together and in nature.

One friend said that when you buy in the city, you buy what is already there (the location, the neighborhood, the schools, a house). Life is established. In the country, you buy potential, or at least that is what he saw us doing. We could change our house, our son's education, our land, our forest. Country life is constantly changing, full of projects, full of new. Clearly, this is a huge

"I feel like I've lived here my entire life."

oversimplification, but there is something to it. Maybe it is merely a reflection of us — of what it took to propel us to who we want to be.

Sometimes we are asked if we have regrets. Of course, we can regret the financial ramifications of our detour to Noble Valley but, well, here we are. We could have owed less on our house. Bought a nicer home. Bought a tractor. Traveled. Struggled less financially. Listened to the Lord more. However, it is a little late for that now. We are the type to reflect and learn from our mistakes, but we do not want to stay in them. That is not who we are.

We hope, too, that our decision to move to the countryside builds strength of character, faith, and body in Jack. Many of us follow the paths set before us during our childhood. While we want Jack to endeavor to whatever he is drawn to, we feel our time invested in him will give him knowledge, character, and a variety of abilities to make his choices more wisely. We offer him skills to aid him in whoever he becomes. *"And these words which I command you today shall be in your heart. You shall teach them diligently to your children, and shall talk of them when you sit in your house, when you walk by the way, when you lie down, and when you rise up"* (Deuteronomy 6: 6–7). We have spent many hours doing mundane chores, homeschooling, and having exciting adventures. All of these build a foundation where he knows how important he is to us. This lifestyle has allowed us to prioritize what is most meaningful for us. Significantly, our family knows one another well.

 https://goo.gl/gJtknT

Homeschooling

During our many moves, Cody and I attempted to keep some normalcy for Jack. He adapted well to repeatedly switching from one bed to another, unsure of what the next day would bring. While we had no real schedule, we continued to homeschool Jack. This provided dedicated time to sit on a couch together to read and talk, focusing on him rather than all of the chaos at hand.

Our initial decision to homeschool was easy and agreeable to both Cody and me. In truth, we discussed it very little. We seemed to know it was the right choice for our family. What we did discuss a great deal was how we were going to homeschool, and if we were doing enough once we started. This discussion was typically prompted by me, as I became the primary teacher. The responsibility to educate Jack felt enormous. Having done it for years now, and sensing I have a grasp on both Jack's schooling and my instructional style, fear of failure still raises its ugly head. I suspect I will never deem my teaching satisfactory until guaranteed he displays genius in all artistic, intellectual, athletic, linguistic, mathematical, and scientific pursuits. Anticipated date: never.

If you are new to homeschooling or alternative education, here are six things to study.

Pros and Cons

Like any endeavour, pros and cons of homeschooling exist. The benefits of home study are significant. The family unit generally strengthens because homeschooling families spend a great deal of time playing and learning together. You get to pick and choose what your children learn and can tailor their education to their personality, needs, and interests. Jack enjoys Lego®s more than your average child. In fact, he has constructed a Lego® village consisting of nearly 40 buildings, which covers a large portion of his bedroom floor. Any money he saves, he spends on Lego®s. Following his great love, I sometimes use Lego®s to teach, whether it involves building Lego® catapults when combining a study of history and physics, or practicing communication skills by sitting back to back describing to the other how to build something based on size, color, space, and direction. It is more difficult than you might imagine.

Homeschooling allows you to delay introducing topics your child is not yet ready to learn cognitively, socially, or developmentally. You can provide in-depth, one-on-one attention in problem areas or areas of particular interest. In addition, you can schedule the day around your routines. A homeschool day is significantly shorter than a classroom day, allowing your child to play more, study specific topics, perform community service, or work around the homestead.

The cons include strangers thinking you and your children must be exceedingly odd. Strangers inevitably ask why your children are not in school, and when you respond "homeschooling," next ask what grade your child is in. Much to Jack's and my amusement, I convinced him at an incredibly young age, say four or five, to answer, "I'm in the eighth grade." We would then start laughing, along with the stranger, and often avoid the socialization question that inevitably would be asked next.

Homeschooling in the treehouse

Another negative effect affects the pocketbook, becoming a one-income family. While homeschooling parents regularly discuss tight budgets, I have never heard anyone say they could not manage it financially. Recently, a friend and I eliminated unnecessary items from her budget so she could quit her job to homeschool. Gone were music lessons, a whole slew of sports activities, dance classes, frequent trips overseas, shopping for fun, and lots of eating out. Her family can still participate in plenty of these activities, but they might not happen in such a carefree manner, or as frequently as they once did.

Other cons include no break from your children. Any free time to shop, exercise, or finish projects while the children attend school vanishes. Your house, if like ours, was always "clean yesterday." The house and its furniture get dirtier and more worn. You created a full-time, non-salaried position for which you receive few daily thanks. Your children will thank you eventually, but usually years later, when they have grown and realize the rewards of homeschooling. Your patience will be tested, if not by how difficult some subjects are to teach, then by the child himself. One day when Jack was being a challenging student, he had a bit of a mischievous grin. I asked him why he was being so troublesome, to which he replied, "Mamma, I'm just pushing your buttons." Indeed, he was. He knows how to make me laugh.

Trust Yourself

Be realistic and trust your judgment. When Jack was roughly three or four years old, we started getting emails entitled, "Teach your toddler to read *Moby Dick* before it is too late," "American children are falling behind. What every Japanese four-year-old already knows, and so should yours," and "Harvard-bound. Proper pre-school education is the ONLY way to secure admission to an Ivy League School. Is your child missing out?" I had not even started homeschooling, yet I had already failed dismally. The pressure was real.

At four, Jack was clearly above average (according to his parents), but no Einstein. He could not solve complex mathematical equations or diagram compound sentences. He wanted to play in his sandbox, be pushed on the swing, and move his Thomas the Train set around. Normal. A normal little boy who learned because he was healthy, secure, and loved. He could not help himself.

Not all education involves reading, writing, and arithmetic. At school, children learn how to give speeches, wait their turn, practice patience, and participate in large group activities. At home you may forgo some of those subjects for others. Your child still learns — simply atypical matters. When he was not yet three, Jack followed Cody and Cody's dad around as they performed various construction projects. He learned not to get underfoot and how to use the various tools.

This fine education became problematic when we were building a fence. Jack stole Cody's drill so habitually we bought him his own seven-volt drill. He was only 28 months old.

At ten years old, Jack has better ax skills than I do (hard to admit). I can send him to the wood shop for a stick with a length of 15 and 3/4 inches and know he can measure and saw it with no problem. Sometimes, as the teacher, you learn what instructions you neglect to deliver. A nail was too long and Cody sent Jack to shorten it. After waiting an exceedingly long time, Cody grew suspicious that something was wrong. Jack emerged with the shortened nail. With perseverance and tenacity, he sawed through the nail, with a brand new carpenter's saw. We were proud of him for taking the initiative, but sad to see the new saw destroyed. Clearly, it was not his fault, but he now knows the difference between a hacksaw and a carpenter's saw.

If we have guests coming, I can hand Jack the recipe for a blueberry crisp and anticipate it will be ready when the guests arrive. His chore list includes vacuuming, mopping, stacking wood, doing dishes, folding laundry — you get the picture. Nothing extraordinary, but as Jack's mother and teacher, my job includes teaching him household duties too. As one friend with numerous boys put it, "I'm raising someone else's husband."

Be realistic about the goals you set for you and your children. Do you honestly remember the characteristics of igneous, sedimentary, and metamorphic rocks? I bet you learned about them in elementary school and then again in junior high science class, but have probably forgotten most, if not all information on rocks' elements. Who is Marquis de Lafayette? You could guess from his name he was a Frenchman, and you may associate the name with Lafayette, Louisiana, but you have likely forgotten why you once learned his name. Think both French and American Revolutionary Wars. Nope, that did not help me either. My point: children learn things more than once. The nitty-gritty details are generally not particularly important. Familiarity of history, literary, and cultural references are essential to learn, but drilling someone with facts does not make them "stick." Do not push your children to learn too many things. Teach fewer subjects than you imagine. Bundle subjects together. A book on Lewis and Clark covers science, history, geography, and reading.

I received a fine education in a public school and personally know many supportive, accommodating, and effective teachers. However, I did find some truth in the following quote, "Education is what remains after one has forgotten what one has learned in school," attributed to Albert

Learning unique skills in the woodshop

Einstein. The education you provide should be the love of learning and how to learn, not the answers to Trivial Pursuit questions. You want your children to pick up books of their own accord because they love them. Two educators I appreciated, a married couple named Raymond and Dorothy Moore, espoused the "better late than early" concept. They vouched for the benefits of learning, but warned parents against pushing concepts and skills before a child was ready. We, as parents, spend the greatest amount of time with our children, and often know best when to push them to try something or when to wait.

Jack is our very own case in point. We must goad him when it comes to physical activities. He moaned and groaned when learning to bike, swim, and ski. He made a valiant effort to wear us down, but we persevered, and refused to relent in pushing him to try. These victorious parents recognize Jack physically can succeed in areas he mentally does not want to tackle. On the flip side, I knew to wait when he experienced difficulty reading.

Jack loved stories and books from a young age. He would listen to us or an audiobook for hours on end while keeping his hands busy doing other things. Because we enjoy classics, his vocabulary grew to include scads of old-fashioned words, garnering chuckles that such large, outdated words should come from such a tiny boy. His friend declared last year, "My mom likes to have you come over. She likes to hear you talk." The worst punishment for him was to take away his books or his DVD player, which he used to listen to his audiobooks. When he was four, and exceedingly grumpy and sleepy, I put all books out of his reach as I strapped him into his carseat hoping he would sleep on the car ride, which he regularly did. He threw a tantrum, cried, and carried on, finally, yelling at me, "You can take away my books but you can't take away my imagination." While driving, I chuckled over and over again at my sleeping boy in the backseat.

As we made our way through basic phonics material and simple reading books, Jack did not seem to remember sounds he had learned moments before. He failed to see cat, rat, hat, and fat were related. He knew his letters. He wanted to read. He patiently tried to sound the words out, but struggled to grasp even the simplest concepts. I did not believe he was slow or had a learning disability or that he would never be able to read. I simply believed it was not his time yet. When he was eight, we still had not finished *Teach Your Child to Read in 100 Easy Lessons*. When he finally figured reading out, it was as if a switch had been flipped. Overnight he became a voracious reader who tackles any book you put in front of him.

Educate Yourself About Homeschooling.

Some families set-up a traditional classroom atmosphere in their home, with children studying in similar conditions to a public school, while others embrace unschooling — the complete opposite, where a child's interests and readiness determine what and how things are learned. You will likely find you start more traditionally and eventually relax, moving to the couch and kitchen table as the years roll by. While much of our homeschooling takes place on the sofa, math happens at the dining room table, where distractions can be limited.

If you decide to unschool, make sure your children learn basic skills in math, reading, writing, and well-known historical and cultural facts. One family I know unschooled their two daughters, completely leaving their education to the young girls. Close in age, the elder decided she might want to attend college, so she taught herself the skills thought necessary. The other lacked certainty about what she wanted to do and never learned even rudimentary skills, which causes many struggles for her as an adult. While such strict implementation of unschooling remains unusual, we, as parents, must teach certain skills that are essential and enjoyable to have later in life.

The library is always the first place we stop when we want to learn about a topic. Read books on homeschooling, education, and child development. Assorted methodologies will be described, which help you determine what suits your child's learning style and your teaching style. Methods are the manner or style in which you teach,

where curriculum is the material you use while teaching. Reading about several teaching methods caused my eyes to glaze over, indicating it might be impossible for me to implement well. If you judge something to be boring, you will find it mind-numbing and excruciating to commit to teaching in that style for hours each day. Homeschooling is fun, but a great deal of work. Do not make it harder than it already will be.

Because both Jack and I love books, curriculums recommending sitting on the couch reading all day were the ones most appealing to us. We both dislike worksheets and fill-in-the-blanks, unlike some children who love them. If you have one who loves them, buy worksheets! In this era of homeschooling, there exists choices for all tastes and learning styles.

To educate yourself further, attend homeschooling conferences. They are both overwhelming and indispensable. I have attended one in particular for close to a decade. I talk to educators and scholars with decades of experience. Almost every hour, numerous lecturers present information on their specialty. I learn about language education, science notebooks, humorous topics, organization, and a whole host of other matters. Additionally, you pick up catalogs over which you later pour for hours. They are an education in themselves. I recommend buying curriculum at the conference and using the catalogs as a reference for future purchases. A problem at our local conference has become that fewer people purchase at the conference, instead waiting for online deals or buying used, resulting in fewer vendors attending. This diminishes both the selection and the sharing of their knowledge on specific topics.

In the main hall, games, books, and other wares can be purchased at discounted rates. Questions can be asked. Our whole family likes to attend. It is encouraging to see parents embrace teaching their children, from the purple-haired mohawk-wearing, tattooed man to the modestly attired, hair-covered woman. We can barely pull Jack away from a special science section. Seven or eight hours of physics are somehow not enough. Curriculum sellers talk on why material should be presented using specific techniques, how music study affects the brain, and why Latin will forever be the best language to learn. One year, an enchanting, elderly, white-haired lady, who was selling her cursive handwriting curriculum, mesmerized Cody. Jack was barely printing at the time, and yet Cody spoke with her at length regarding the importance of handwriting educa-tion. A few years later, guess what has been introduced to our curriculum now that Jack is older?

Education – a family
responsibility

I am acquainted with one woman who wears pink-tinted lenses in her
glasses. She always struggled in school and feared taking on the role of
teacher to her children, but decided to try homeschooling. She attended
a homeschooling conference, browsing at a variety of booths, when she
met a man selling something related to learning disabilities. The man
showed her some of the tests he gave children to determine if there might
be anything from which they suffered. As she peered through a pink
looking glass, she stood there dumbfounded. She asked the man how he
had gotten the letters on the page to stop moving. They quickly realized
that she, the teacher, had an undiagnosed eye problem she had lived with
her entire life. For most of her life, she considered herself intellectually
slow. She saw an eye doctor and now feels bright, capable, and confident.
I love that story and have heard her relate it more than once. You may
learn something at a homeschooling conference you never expected.

Join a co-op or homeschool group

We signed up for the email lists of two vastly diverse homeschool groups
in the area. One organizes a weekly homeschool co-op, where parents
teach and children choose three classes to attend for an hour each.
Years ago, we joined a similar co-op at a separate location and the level
of teaching was phenomenal. Because of distance, we recently started
attending this new co-op. Classes vary from Indian culture, computer
programming, dessert making, and fire science to invertebrate zoology.

Because this was Jack's first year and he knew few of the children, I let him choose from the "less demanding" classes. He chose field hockey, art, and Lego® building. I help in two of his classes and admit I love it when they need an extra player in field hockey!

The other homeschool group meets for weekly Nerf® battles. More accurately, it meets for approximately two hours of calmer play followed by two hours of adrenaline-filled physicality. Mainly boys, from 9 to 14 years old, who run themselves ragged.

Both groups plan field trips, including theater visits, fish hatchery tours, and museum outings. In addition to the educational aspect of the groups, it provides a venue to interact with other families and ask questions regarding curriculum, testing, child development, and a whole host of other issues popping up when you homeschool.

Alternatives

If you are uncertain about taking the plunge to homeschool, look into some of the public school alternatives. We enrolled in a program put on by our state. It allowed us to choose from several curriculum options sent to us, that we used at home to teach Jack. The program required us to submit weekly reports on his learning, as well as take standardized testing. For several reasons, we decided it was not a great fit for us, but a number of friends participate in the program, or similar programs, depending upon where they live. Other friends receive curriculum and lesson plans from a public school they attend only once a week, home studying the other days of the week. Both parents and children attend together to ensure the parents know what the schoolteacher has already taught and has for expectations. The public school alternative gives curriculum, guidance, and accountability. You can often tailor the curriculum to meet your needs. However, you do not experience the freedom and flexibility which homeschooling provides.

Patience

You do not need to have unlimited patience to homeschool, only resolve. This is not completely true, but too many people give up before even trying. Granted, it is not for everyone. I know three women who homeschool only two of their three children. Each has a child for whom school was a better choice this year. One child has been homeschooled until this year but now attends a two-room schoolhouse with an extremely experienced teacher. The girl loves to be around other children her age, is constantly on the go, and her parents sensed the two younger children would benefit from alone time with mom. The other girl, age ten, hates to be alone or work independently. She has attended both public and private schools, and receives praise for her schoolwork and good behavior. However, when at home, her parents detected something seemed amiss, have been unable to determine why, and plan to homeschool her next year. The third family uses a combination of homeschooling and public school for their youngest son. He was being disrespectful to the mother and they were having difficulty curtailing the behavior. The mother wanted a break and they put him into school for half days. Their relationship has improved, and the boy has requested to return to homeschooling full-time next year. No situation is perfect for everyone. Make decisions based on what suits your family's needs, abilities, and time in life. You can change things from year to year.

Make sure you comply with your homeschooling laws. These laws vary from state to state and country to country. Homeschooling is illegal, with severely limited or no exceptions, in numerous countries. Some that may surprise include Brazil, Sweden, Germany, Greece, Iceland, The Netherlands, Luxemburg, and Spain. It is a right and privilege many of us take for granted. Check out HSLDA as a starting point for more information.

Learn more about the state laws regarding homeschooling.

 https://goo.gl/nqezoU

better. And yes, it is true that a lot of the work you or I will do, as we are learning, is never as good as we want it to be. But that doesn't mean that you shouldn't strive for it to be perfect, to get as close to the lines as you can, or get your joints as tight as possible. Eventually, you will get there.

There are so many spiritual lessons in this as well. Whatever we may do — working in an office, writing code, or stone masonry — God tells us to do everything to the glory of Him. The Bible tells us to do everything to the glory of God. That means cutting straight on a line, that means

keeping our home, office, or car clean, and taking care of these important things. All of these things are lessons, or can be lessons, to be excellent wherever you are or whatever you're doing. This should be our endeavor.

Checking, Crowns, & Wane

Checking is just part of timber framing. Just because the timber has a crack doesn't mean it is structurally compromised and cannot be used. It will still be strong. It won't hurt anything, because timber framing involves overbuilding everything. Just put the crack to the inside.

The crown is a slight natural rise or dip in the wood — you can see it by sighting along its length from the end of the timber like a gun barrel. Some timber will have more than others. Crown everything and always put the crown up — over time, the weight of a wall, or its use as part of the floor, will even it up. You do not want to have a crown that dips in the wood on anything load bearing.

Wane is the rough or missing edges of the timber due to bark removal on the corner or edge of the wood. You can use a

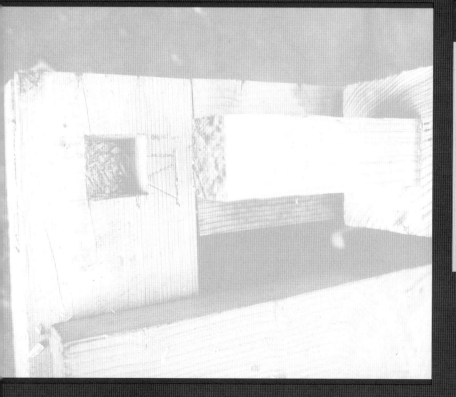

Helpful Hint:

Timber framing joints means, essentially, that each one is a customized fit. That is why I mark the two timbers, where the joints are joined, with Roman numerals, so that I know they go together if the project is ever disassembled.

draw knife to smooth out the edges if it is rough. Again, wane, like checking, will not impact the structural integrity of the timber. Keep your hard clean edges (no wane) to the top, putting blemished edges to the bottom. It shows pride in craftsmanship.

Turn any blemishes like checking or wane to the inside where they cannot be seen, as part of good craftsmanship. Even if this portion of the project won't be seen, put your best foot forward by removing planer marks or other imperfections. Always think of knotholes as holes in the wood. They are weak points, even on newly cut wood, because eventually the wood will dry and the knot will fall out and leave a hole.

Making Your Mark

When you have two timbers that are not exactly the same dimensions, you have to make compromises. You have to have two sides that are flush for the joint, so you have to make up the differences in some way. You can do that with the bottom and inside of the timbers, but you want a flush, flat top and on the outside where they join. This is so siding or other coverings on the corners will lay flat. You can always shim the bottom and ignore the inside dimension difference.

For a tongue and fork joint, you determine the length of the mortice because of the width of the timber that will be joined with it is the tenon. For example, if the tenon timber width is 6.5 inches, then the mortice will need to be 6.5 inches in length.

Then, you need to mark the timbers on the sides where cuts will be made. This is very important. It can save you hours when it is done right. I use a tape measure to make a small mark with a razor knife. When you compare the width of a pencil line and a razor knife blade, you can see how tight and precise the mark of the razor knife is. A pencil width really varies, and if you are on either side of the line, before you know it you are 1/8 or 1/32 off.

Put the razor knife in the mark you have made, and then slide the metal square up against the blade. Hold the square down firmly and mark across the timber using the knife. The mark will be hard to see, so take a sharp point pencil and mark with it inside the shallow groove made by the knife. If you use a carpenter's pencil, make sure you have a nice sharp point. I use the razor knife to cut back the wood and then rotate the pencil as I sharpen the point. Some carpenters use mechanical pencils, that isn't a bad idea either.

Time for the Tenon

When you are preparing to cut off excess wood on the end to form the tenon, it is best to mark the areas to be removed in pencil with a large "X" on all sides so you can easily see what you are doing. This is so there is no question about what is to be removed. When you are adjusting the depth of your cut, leave 3/16 to 1/4 of an inch and finish with a hand saw or hand tool, keeping away from the lines.

Making the Cut

Before making the initial rough cuts, take your skill saw and set the fence on the top of the timber, positioning the blade against the side of the timber where you have marked. This way you can adjust the depth of the blade and visually see how close you are getting to the line. As I noted earlier, it is best that you leave a little space before the line to be safe. How much space is left will depend on your proficiency with the saw.

Next, use the saw to cut a series of notches divided across the width of the wood marked as needing to be removed for the tenon only on the top and bottom of the timber. For a tongue and fork joint, you do not cut the sides of the timber forming the tenon. On the tenons, I always cut to the line, leaving the line visible. On the mortices, I cut into the line. It's easy to make a mistake and you need to be sure before you begin cutting. As they say, measure twice and cut once, because large timbers are hard-fought and difficult to come by. For me, to go from tree to timber, it takes an entire day to yield four to six timbers. If you miss the mark and improperly cut, you are not going to find a replacement at your local lumberyard.

Cutting out the Mortice

For the mortice, you cut from the end into the length of the timber with the skill saw on two sides and the front of the timber's end. You will be removing the middle portion of the wood so the tenon will fit into it. You can use a carpenter's saw to finish the cuts to get closer to the markings. Reverse the

By hand or power saw?

If you choose to use a skill saw for the initial rough cuts to the timber, you have to be careful. These saws are fast and efficient, but if you make a mistake, it happens quickly and cannot be undone. The timbers can be easily ruined for your project, though they can be trimmed back and later used for other projects.

drill to remove the bit from the wood. Do both the top and bottom of the timber this way.

You can also use the 1.5-inch auger-style drill bit to speed up the process of removing the unwanted wood. Measure from the inside of the cut mark on the timber of the mortice, half the width of the bit or 3/4-inch. This way the drill bit will run precisely down the back of the mortice. You can do it all by hand with the chisels, but it very laborious.

Chipping Away

Make sure the timber is cribbed up at a height that is comfortable for you to work on. I use saw ponies that I made because they are sturdy.

Position the timber so the wood to be worked with the chisel is at the top. Use a mallet and chisel to start chipping away the excess wood on the tenon, trying to stay within the markings on the timber. Don't start on the line — go a little above to begin the initial chipping out of the notched chunks on the top and bottom. Once the large chunks are removed, you can begin working closer to the lines.

You can control the precision of your work much better with the chisels than by using power tools. I like to use the 1.5-inch chisel for this part of the process. It has a better weight than the 2-inch. Be sure to have the beveled edge against the face of the wood — it helps you control the depth of the cut. You don't want to work with the bevel up and the back of the chisel on the book unless you don't care about the depth of the cut or the precision needed.

Lightly tap the chisel with the mallet to remove smaller portions of the wood closer to the marked lines. Use the slick to really smooth off the face of the tenon. You never pound on the handle of the slick. It is strictly to be used by hand. The width of the tool lets you get a nice broad cutting edge that knocks down the high spots.

Properly sharpened, the slick will produce thin shavings. Always sheath the chisel when you are not working with it.

Coming Together

When it is time to fit the joints together, be sure you are matching the correct pairs of timbers and mark the pair if you haven't done so. I use my chisel to notch in the Roman numerals. You can use the deadblow hammer and ratchet straps to slowly position and to tap them into place. They should fit tightly and firmly without any glue or nails. For some different types of joints, you would use treenails or pegs to help finish it.

Different Kinds of Joints

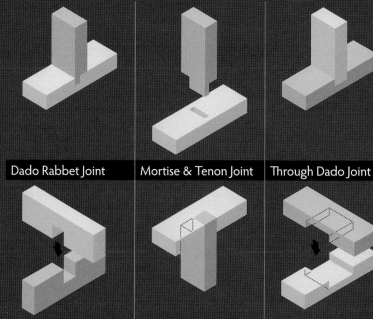

Dado Rabbet Joint | Mortise & Tenon Joint | Through Dado Joint

Edge Cross Lap Joint | Half Cross Lap Joint | Tee Lap Joint

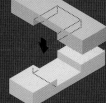

Final Note

There isn't enough room to talk about all the aspects of timber framing in this book, but there are a number of videos available at our Wranglerstar channel on YouTube that you can use to learn the basics of several techniques. There is even a set showing how to timber frame a cabin. You can find them in the playlist section of the site.

Remember, you don't have to be planning to build a large structure to use these skills. They apply to a number of tasks you may want to try in your home, on your homestead, or as part of small crafts or hobbies.

Wranglerstar:

Why do I put so much time and effort into this? As the world becomes more homogenous, I think my inner man just strives and fights against that, and wants to have some kind of connection to the past, something that gives me an identity.

Building Things That Last

Many older skills, such as ax sharpening, dovetailing, timber framing, and tool restoration, are reemerging as interesting and useful. We scour antique and thrift stores to find old-fashioned tools and kitchen staples. More accurately, we call this a date. We set a budget, head to the store, part at the door with a kiss, and later meet to inspect each other's prospective purchases. If clothing is bought, a fashion show occurs later at home. Jack has now reached the age where he wants part of the budget. Family fun, on the cheap. In addition to the thrill of the hunt, we like to learn new things, but also enjoy the quietness that often accompanies traditional ways to accomplish things.

An example of the beauty of using traditional methods is wanting to drill a hole in a piece of wood a mile or so away. The old-fashioned way, you grabbed your hand-drill, walked, accompanied by your dog, to

Craftsmanship is a big part of learning woodworking skills.

where the piece of wood waited. You positioned the drill and hand-cranked it, boring out the desired hole. The walk took you 20 minutes each way, so your job took about 45 minutes, plus you got some exercise and made your dog happy.

In a modern situation, you grab your cordless drill and walk to your truck. You then realize you left your keys in the house and go back to find them. Return to the truck. Start the truck and head to your destination. While driving there, you hit a soft spot and your tire digs in deep. You try forward and reverse but get stuck deeper. You climb out of your truck and lock the wheels into four-wheel drive. You climb back into the truck and pull forward. You arrive, park, and turn off the truck. You grab your drill and approach the spot where the hole is supposed to go. Rats! The battery is dead.

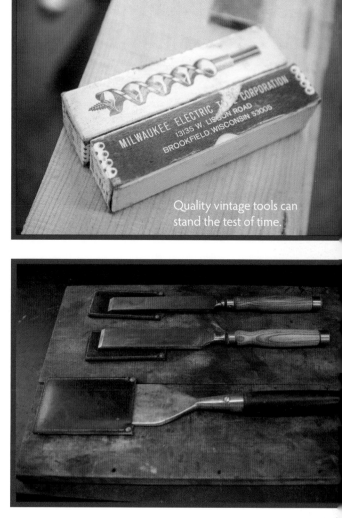

Quality vintage tools can stand the test of time.

Now you need to head back to your shop to grab a new battery (hopefully you left one charging) or you need to grab your electric drill, plus the generator to power it. You climb into the truck, reverse, and drive back home. Fortunately, you charged the extra battery, so you grab it and climb into your truck and head back to where the hole waits to be drilled. You arrive and exit the vehicle, drill in hand. You bore the hole. Noisy. Again, you climb back into truck. You drive home. An hour has passed. The dog waits on the porch for you to take him on his walk.

Yes, an exaggeration, but truth can be found. We enjoy working in the forest best when we turn off the power tools. We like to keep it quiet in the "Quietwoods," what we dubbed one forest. As we cleared the forest of limbs and such we stepped on something hard, which turned out to be a sign saying Quietwoods. Cody made posts from some saplings we cleared

The sign says it all.

and the sign now marks the entrance to that section of forest. Sometimes we use power tools, but usually we do not. Another overlooked aspect of using vintage tools is the enormous cost savings they can present. Unlike vintage tools, engines have a relatively short life span, which seems to be getting shorter and shorter. Do not get me wrong — tools with small engines can be a tremendous help on the homestead. Just remember that this convenience comes with a cost. Vintage tools, on the other hand, can be over 150 years old and do not deteriorate if maintained. In many cases, a properly restored, sharpened, vintage hand tool is as productive as a modern electric machine. Old tools were meant to be purchased once, providing quality and value for a lifetime. Many handsaws made now cannot be sharpened at home because of the way the teeth are cut, whereas a vintage saw can be sharpened by anyone, and lasts for generations.

Timber Framing and Chainsaw Milling

Cody started timber framing in 2010. Once we made the decision to adopt a homesteading way of life, Cody realized the importance of learning the age-old method of timber frame construction. The appeal lay in building barns or homes without using electricity or multiple trips to the hardware store for supplies manufactured by someone else. The structures represent a self-sufficiency and beauty. For thousands of years,

Cody operates his chainsaw mill with the guide.

man used basic hand tools to go from tree to timber to structure. It is truly astonishing that with a small toolbox, containing no more than a dozen tools, a person can construct a building completely out of wood using no nails, screws, or fasteners of any sort. Armed with timber frame books from the library and a few second-hand tools acquired from our former neighbor, Cody began timber framing.

Once we purchased Noble Valley, Cody began milling his own timbers to use. While terminology differs across the globe, in the United States, lumber is wood that is processed into beams and planks, whereas timber refers to wood immediately after being felled, as well as lumber six inches in its smallest dimension. To mill timber, Cody first began by cutting down a tree, preferably one with few branches or crooks. Then he limbed the log, with either an ax or chainsaw, depending upon its dimension. He would use his pee-vee to roll the log in order to limb the underside. Then, he bucked the log into usable lengths. Next, he debarked the log with a bark spud. He did this because wind-blown sand and debris collects in bark, which is exceedingly abrasive on a saw blade. His chainsaw mill, the Alaskan Chainsaw mill, is not the most efficient way to mill lumber, but it is portable, affordable, and uses the chainsaw he already owned.

Once the logs were milled, he loaded them in his truck and drove them to Riverview. Mornings and evenings, he notched and planed the timbers, starting a little cabin we planned to construct at Noble Valley.

Preparing to join a tongue and fork joint

Using the slick to smooth out the rough places

He lovingly put the timbers together in his shop. Plenty of evenings, we stood in our "cabin," imagining where it would eventually stand, with windows and a little stove, facing the mountain view. When we sold Riverview, we stored many things in our former neighbor's yard, including the timber frame cabin, half of which stayed on our trailer. While we developed the off-grid property, we used Cody's truck with its lumber rack for hauling — no need for the trailer. Finally closing on the homestead, we realized we needed the trailer to empty our storage lockers. We unloaded the trailer of its timber frame load in one of the homestead's outbuildings and went to retrieve more boxes, furniture, and other items. Upon our return, we saw the cabin had been taken. Stolen. Gone. It was a shocking start to our move to the homestead.

I literally felt sick to my stomach. Cody spent hundreds of hours on the timber framed cabin. Every piece was hand-milled, hand-cut, handmade. He has since remilled everything stolen, but it sits waiting for windows, roof, and floor. The budget often dictates when projects are completed. Cody attempted to reassemble it recently. Unfortunately, ignored, the timbers warped, adding to our disappointment. On the bright side, we can mill the timbers into something else, and on Cody's next effort he will have more skill than before.

We suspect the homestead sat empty for so long that unthinking, sticky-fingered individuals became accustomed to rummaging around for things they thought no longer belonged or mattered to the previous owners. They likely judged theft from a bank as not being theft at all. They were wrong on two counts — it was theft, no matter who owned the homestead, and it mattered dearly to us. Neither the timbers nor the thieves have returned.

Bees

We decided to keep bees. We knew nothing, except we suspected I was allergic to them. Years earlier, I had been stung by an unidentified source. So strong was my reaction, I could not put my leg into my pants due to swelling. Eventually, I took steroids to return my leg to its normal size. I carry an epi-pen. Besides a few other basics, like honey, pollination, queen bee, and worker bee, my reaction was the extent of our knowledge. Not surprisingly, I felt less enthusiasm than Cody did about getting bees.

Nonetheless, we checked out bee books from the library. After studying, we chose to construct a top-bar beehive. Like many of our other projects, funds were non-existent, so we used scrap wood to build and set the completed hive in the orchard. One morning, Cody rushed in to say we must leave immediately. It was bee delivery day. Our package of bees

A reminder that faith is a part of our daily lives.

Cody at the
bee hive

was ready for pick up. The beekeeper was in a rush, so we frantically threw questions his way. Somehow, the responsibility of the buzzing box weighed enormously.

The drive home was uncomfortable. Unwittingly, in our hurry, we took the SUV and not the truck. One piece of information we obtained from the beekeeper was the bees would be furious until settled into the hive. As one would expect, I suffered a wee bit of paranoia sharing the vehicle with a box of bees. I remained silent, my normal reaction when worried and unable to do anything about it. Cody, laissez faire, said not to worry about it. We would simply roll down the windows. I tightly gripped my epi-pen. Once home, we regarded the box with curiosity. How does one convince irritated, enraged bees to come out of a box?

Jack and Cody suited up in bee suits. Jack had on an adult suit, so duct tape was used to secure the legs and arms. Cody ventured out without the requisite bee pants, instead wearing tin pants. Tin pants are Filson's water repellent pants made of cotton. Cody has worn them for roughly 25 years. He can wear the same pair for a year or two. You cannot wash them. Gross. He can literally lean them against the wall. He knows not to sit on any furniture in them. On a positive note, it cuts down on laundry. So far, tin pants remain impervious to bee stings. I stood outside of the orchard fence, with my running shoes on, ignoring Cody's calls to come nearer and videotape.

With the top of the hive open, Cody took the lid off the cardboard box, tipped it upside down, and vigorously shook the box. He literally poured the bees into the hive, much like water from a pitcher. He closed the lid and ran, following after Jack. Hours later, the angry mass of bees settled down. In the evening, we looked inside the hive. Cody had installed a viewing window in the hive to watch the bees build comb. The queen bee was not yet installed. We received her in a little package called an introduction cage. We were instructed to place the package between two frames and the worker bees would chew her out. Apparently, when introducing the queen, she will be killed if they fail to become accustomed to her scent. Fascinating. It has been said that once you make the decision to keep bees, you never look at the world the same.

Crosscut Saws

Cody has developed a deep respect for crosscut saws. He loves to handle them, saw with them, and sharpen them. When we chose the location for our garden, we suspected that three trees would likely need to come down. No matter what location we chose, something was shading the garden. It happens when you live in the forest. We chose to use a two-person felling saw to cut down the ugly, enormous Douglas fir. It was scraggly and crooked — I was not sad to see it go. I had only been on the end of a saw a few times and all for play prior to this experience. A felling saw is lighter and more flexible than a bucking saw. The felling saw is used to fall a tree, while a bucking saw is used to cut the log into manageable sections. Bucking saws are heavier and a bit more ridged. This allows gravity to come into play. The additional weight aids the sawyer (logger) in cutting faster, and the stiffness prevents binding on the push stroke. The sawyer, while felling, must support the weight of the saw while cutting, so weight is a consideration. The felling saw also has a concave back, which allows a wedge to be put in sooner to prevent the tree from pinching the saw if it decides to sit back on the stump.

The tree to come down stood 125 feet high and four feet in diameter. Before felling, Jack joined us and we girdled the tree with axes, which is to chop the bark away around the entire tree where the saw will cut. Bark holds things that dull or damage the saw blade, like dirt, screws, and nails put in for birdhouse and laundry lines you usually cannot see. If the tree stands near a house, wager money it is full of that type of steel. Cody uses a metal detector before milling any sort of tree harvested near a house or barn.

Because I am significantly shorter than Cody, I stood on the uphill side when we were ready to saw. We both grabbed our ends and began a back and forth movement before the blade even touched the tree. You want to establish a rhythm allowing the saw to "sing," to hum along. The blade grabbed hold and the noodles started flying. Noodles are the woodcarvings flying from the tree. The blade has cutting teeth and raker teeth. The raker teeth rake the cut fibers out of the cut, depositing them at the base of the tree. You want noodles instead of small shards or scraps of wood, as it means your blade is sharp and your technique is proficient. Noodles stopped flying occasionally and we would need to pull the saw out and begin the rocking movement again. Sometimes we lost our rhythm, sometimes one person pushed or pulled too hard. Usually you only apply pressure when you pull the saw, but this husband and wife team admits to a little pressure put on during the husband's push. It was the polite thing to do. We paused now and again to make certain it would fall in the right direction. Dropping to the east could destroy Cody's wood shop, the garden shed, and part of the house. In the other direction stood the century-old homesteader barn and orchard. The other direction would block access to our big barn. There was only one spot to lay it down. It

Using a cross cut saw

was exciting to stand beneath the limbs and look up. I only knew that wherever it dropped, I wanted to be headed in the opposite direction. I have been told that logging and commercial fishing are the two most dangerous jobs around, but I told myself this was somehow different. This was an experience to be savored. The majority of people never cut down a tree of this size, much less with a crosscut saw and their spouse. Four hours after we began girdling, the ground shook as the immense tree took its last bow. Truly exhilarating. We laughed with pent-up emotion and relief. Cody was so proud of me.

That ragged, oversized tree contributed to several assorted projects on the homestead. The main section of the trunk was milled into timbers for the second timber frame cabin and a treehouse for Jack. The branches, because of their density, will heat our home for months. The needles and branches, too small for firewood, were chipped and mulched, and used in our garden. The sawdust was collected, some put in the compost and some in Cody's shop for soaking up spills that occur. Even the pinecones were collected by Jack for pinecone village — an elaborate community he created from sticks, pinecones, dirt, and water from the hose. I will admit the last time we were at the lumberyard, Cody said something about purchasing some additional lumber, and I told him he should mill his own. He shook his head and laughed but came home and milled some boards from the timber.

We do not cut down trees lightly. When forests are unhealthy and nothing grows well, something must be done. Some say to let nature

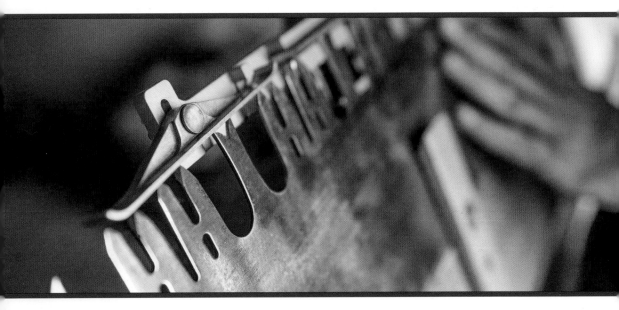

do its thing but, frankly, we try to avoid wildfires racing through our forest, close to our home. Even those who want a "wild" yard, still pull or cut back weeds, cut a path to the front door, and manage their property, even if minimally. The forest craves

Crosscut saw in action

management too. In the past, wildfire came through forests every seven to ten years, cleaning out underbrush and little trees. They happened frequently, moving quickly through the forest. Today, firefighters are so proficient at putting out fires, that forests do not receive frequent burns, and so become overgrown and unhealthy. Bushes, limbs, and small trees provide fuel when a wildfire does come through. There is often so much of this fuel that a fire gains much more intensity than if fires happened more frequently. In the past, larger trees could survive the less intense, quick-moving fire, but now the intensity of the fires kills the big trees too. We like our big trees, which is why we limb and trim in our forest.

The forest service and smoke jumpers still actively use crosscut saws. Chainsaws are generally not allowed in national forests. Lugging gas and protective equipment, plus the weight of the chainsaw itself, is cumbersome. Crosscut saws are easier to use. Felling saws are flexible enough to be bent over a horse-pack or backpack thrown out of a plane. They regain their shape when released. Pretty incredible.

Cody became so intrigued with all things crosscut that he actually attended a five-day, crosscut saw sharpening course at the Nine Mile Ranger Station in Montana. The classroom was packed with lovers of detail and tedium. Forty hours of saw sharpening with files, requiring precise measuring is not up my alley, but Cody loved it. When sharpened properly, a blade saws an entire summer out in the forest.

After the class, Cody built a vise specifically for crosscut saw sharpening. As an amateur sharpener, one saw takes him roughly eight hour to complete. Old-timers hired by logging camps were allotted an hour per saw. It has been said if you were a professional sawyer you wanted to be on the good side of the saw filer, because he could make or break you. He was the most pampered man in the camp. If you treated him well, say with a bottle of whiskey or a pie, you were likely to receive a sharp, fine-cutting saw. When you did piece work, per tree, not by the hour, a sharp saw meant money in your pocket and food on your table. If you got on the wrong side of the saw filer, you might expect to receive a saw not quite as sharp as you expected. This latter saw was called a misery whip. Felling timber with a crosscut saw was, and is, so physically demanding, the old time loggers, when too tired to pull any longer, would rest by switching to an ax.

Cody owns numerous saws, but his favorite goes by Wanda. Saws are named after women, and Wanda was named after his Nana. Fittingly, he received the saw from his granddad, Nana's husband. His granddad grew up in Oklahoma, among those who left during the dust bowl. He progressed from being a prairie farmer to a lumberjack in the forests of Idaho. Necessity called and they converted their Model A into a sawmill. One of the first tools purchased was an Atkins crosscut saw. Years later, Cody would help at Nana and Granddad's annual garage sale. Each year, Granddad took that saw off the wall of the garage and put a sticker with $100 on it. Cody would shake his head and wonder at the "old obsolete piece of junk" his granddad once again over-priced. Later it would be one of the last things Cody received from his granddad. It still had the price tag on it — but it was priceless to Cody.

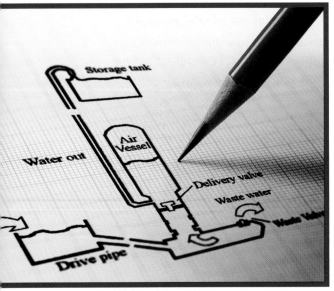

Hydraulic Ram Pump

The ram pump is very old technology that uses the momentum of water to pump. It is simple, reliable, and moves water without fuel, electricity, or solar power and can be built very inexpensively. It uses gravity and the kinetic energy of moving water to create pressure, which in turn moves water. Water funnels through a pipe from an uphill water source until it reaches the ram pump, which contains two valves.

As more and more water flows through the pipe, it increases in speed and eventually "catches" the "waste" valve located in the pump, thereby closing it. The oncoming water continues to surge, developing great pressure behind the waste valve. This pressure forces the water two ways: first, through a spring-loaded check valve and, second, backward into the on-rushing water. This alleviates the pressure at the waste valve, causing the waste valve to re-open and the spring-loaded check valve to close, trapping the water in a delivery pipe. This pipe delivers water away from the pump to the desired location, which can even be uphill. The water traveling down the pipe causes this cycle to repeat itself again and again. The steady rhythmic pounding noise this cycle makes is often referred to as a "water hammer" because of similarity to a hammer pounding on a nail being driven through wood.

Our hydraulic ram pump

Efficiency of the ram pump is not great. The higher the fall from the inlet to the pump, the higher and farther your water travels. Much depends upon how high the water source is above the ram, the length of the inlet pipe, and how high and far the water is pumped. Based on what we have read, only five to ten percent of the water actually makes it to the delivery location — the rest is spilled at the pump via the waste valve. Thus, if you have a creek or a river, you essentially leave the water in the water source, diverting only the smallest amount. You can use either PVC pipes or steel for the inlet pipe, although efficiency increases if the pipe is steel. Efficiency also improves if you solidly mount the inlet pipe and ram pump. This increases the "hammer" pressure, helping the pump to function better. The beauty of the ram pump is it functions where terrain is rather flat or only slightly hilly. There are other alternatives for low water situations or mountainous terrain. Because the pumps need only two moving parts (the check valves) they are simple and inexpensive to maintain. Hard to beat that.

https://goo.gl/Fpkds8

How Are You Going to Pay for That?

Many wonder how to pay for life in the country. It is true — many rural communities lack a wide selection of jobs. Would you consider picking up odd jobs with no stable source of income? To make a living in the country, contemplate out-of-the-box possibilities. One neighbor makes boats. Another builds guitars. Another collects owl pellets to sell. Unless you have an income source, it is an ugly reality that many people sell their property within the first five years. Income is a very important consideration.

In making our way to the homestead, we made both wise and foolish financial decisions. One matter was certain — we had not saved enough to buy a house outright or retire early. Cody ran an at-home business and this allowed us to transition to wherever we wanted to live (within limits). We required Internet access, phone service, and mail service within a reasonable distance. At Noble Valley, the reasonable distance took approximately 45 minutes to drive, in good weather. Reasonable can be pretty subjective.

Most farmers and ranchers work off-property jobs to support their rural lifestyle. The majority of the costs associated with urban living follows you to the countryside. Below are some creative solutions to keep income coming in. Some of the suggestions require government permits or licenses, depending upon where you live. Look into it!

Keep Your Job

For countless individuals, commuting to a steady job in the city is an obvious choice. If your family moves to a new community, a new house, and new school, some stability might be welcome. While so many other areas of your life are in flux, a known income source might alleviate other stresses you will inevitably experience.

While commuting may be a slog, consider the benefits. Instead of driving through city traffic for 45 minutes, would an hour through the country-side be so unpleasant? Ask if you can change your job schedule from five eight-hour days to four ten-hour days. I know one man who rides a van an hour and a half each way to work. He gets reading time and his wife does not worry about him driving while tired. He has multiple children, earns good money, and thinks the benefit of living in a small town makes the commute worthwhile. One acquaintance drives two hours for a 72-hour shift, taking the rest of the week off. We know several firefighters who commute into the big city for extended shifts, but receive five to six days off at a time. Ten days of work a month does not sound so bad.

Can you telecommute a few days a week or even full-time? Make sure you have reliable Internet and phone service before you receive permission to telecommute. Additionally, ensure you receive service in the room where you set up your office. Our Internet connection functions best downstairs, and cell phone reception works best in one of the upstairs bedrooms. Tricky when I need both at the same time. If still reluctant to ask, suggest telecommuting or a condensed schedule on a temporary basis. If it does not work, you can resume a regular schedule. Your employers will never say yes if you hesitate to ask.

On or from the Farm

If you picture yourself to be a small-scale farmer, selling lettuce, berries, and tomatoes at the local market, realize it is an unlikely way to make enough money. You will find countless sellers grow, harvest, and sell as a hobby, because they love it, selling below production cost. It makes it tough to compete. If you produce large quantities at regular intervals, you might be able to skip the famers' markets and go directly to local grocery stores and restaurants. Consider selling plant starts, where you grow from seed to an immature plant and then sell. You get to grow plants and make a profit, but forgo the responsibility to water, fertilize, harden them off, transplant, hope the weather holds out, and harvest.

Generally, you make more with value-added products than plain fruits and vegetables. Value-added means making bread from wheat, sauer-kraut from cabbage, soap from milk, or cheese from milk — anything requiring processing. Will you get tourists who want items that travel well, like jars of jams, bags of beef jerky, or hand-knit objects? While there is time and money spent in adding value, your dollars earned

Mrs. Wranglerstar
working in the garden

increase dramatically. Many states do not insist on using a commercial kitchen if your total sales qualify you as a cottage industry. If you require a commercial kitchen, check about renting one at local community colleges, schools, community centers, and churches.

Is there an interest in a vegetable, meat, or dairy CSA in your community? A CSA is community-shared agriculture, where individuals pay a farmer at the beginning of the season and then receive regular shares of the produce. It is a risk model, so if the harvest is bountiful the individuals receive larger shares, but the opposite can play out too. One CSA owner we know realized the share-buyers did not know how to prepare unusual vegetables, so now includes recipes. Radishes were intimidating. They also streamlined their garden to grow mainly common vegetables to meet this local demand. Another individual in our area is attempting to start a whole meal CSA by coordinating the efforts of local bakers, ranchers, and dairy and orchard farmers, to name a few. The individual must coordinate getting the food together (bread, cheese, meats, herbs, flowers) from the local producers, separate the products into each buyers' shares, deal with pickups or drop-offs of the shares, and then distribute profits to the producers of the goods. A complex endeavor, benefitting numerous small-scale farmers if it succeeds.

If you decide to raise animals and birds for meat and profit, consider the financial investments before you begin. Animals cost money to fence, house, doctor, and raise. However, if you are not terrifically picky about the breed, plenty of animals can be had free. When Cody's parents saw our barn for the first time, they searched Craigslist for animals. Advertised were free horses, alpacas, cows, chickens, pigs, goats, and more, all for the taking. We explained we were not yet looking to populate our homestead with furry creatures, but we now know where to go for free animals.

The friends we mentioned earlier, who suggested getting lambs or goats instead of a lawn mower, followed their own suggestion. They obtained healthy, young stock off Craigslist and other local sources. The first year they ran four pigs around their five acres of pasture and oak trees. The pigs gently tilled the soil, dug up poison oak and other undesirable plants, and left manure to fertilize the soil. In so doing, they also took care of fire suppression issues, which are required by law where they live. The pigs ate acorns from the oaks and nothing else, until they were ready for butchering. Our friends later ate, bartered, or sold their low-cost

pork. Their farm profits (along with some produce sales they had) helped them establish three years of the record keeping required to qualify for an agricultural tax deferment on their property taxes. It also provided recent proof of agricultural experience to qualify for an agriculture loan to put in some infrastructure. The second year they ran four lambs during the summer and fall months without any purchased feeds whatsoever. These low-feeder animals again provided lawn mowing, fire suppression, and tasty meat. I can attest. Overall, for both the pigs and lambs, it cost them $1.00/lb. for pasture-raised, all natural meat. Of course, they provided the labor to check on them and fill up the waterers daily (roughly 15 minutes/day). Later, they also butchered them with some friends and made cured meat and sausages.

Other at-home, in-the-mud possibilities include u-pick berries, apples, or Christmas trees. Corn mazes and pumpkin patches remain a fall tradition. People drive long distances if the location and drive make it worth their while. People enjoy the opportunity to pick berries, press cider, or saw down trees. They missed the upfront labor, but get to enjoy the harvest. Some people have never spent time in the country and would love to come for a farm-to-table dinner, a mushroom scavenging adventure, to learn how to gather roots, for education on how to build almost anything, or to spend a day with farm animals. You can also provide hotel-type accommodations or camping adventures. You would be amazed at how many people have camped on our property for adventure, while for us it is simply daily life. Of course, we prefer a bed to sleeping on the ground while at home.

Handyman

If you possess skills in the trades, you might perform basic mechanical, construction, and plumbing jobs to make a living. If you are also creative, you can take your skills one step further. Can you strip ramshackle barns and make furniture to sell? Do you own a chainsaw mill? How about milling specialty lumber for the area? Can you produce timber fast enough to sell? If your timber is oversized, it usually does not require certification for building permit purposes. Certain larger sizes are exempt. Maybe you can weld? Let people know about your skills. Machinery and tools always break in the country. If you can design a portable welder, people will call you first because of the convenience you bring. Even if you are not the best around, if you can come to their trouble, they may call you for your machinery. If you own a bulldozer or backhoe, you can always find business.

Writing

Blogs saturate the Internet with advice on everything from cars to permaculture to cooking to farming. If you possess a specialty and can write effectively, consider submitting articles to magazines or others' blogs or even start your own. While you may not make much money initially, income can grow quickly. An example of a profitable blog is the food blog Pinchofyum.com. They report their monthly income online. In roughly four years, they went from spending money to a gross profit of around $30,000/month. Clearly, their costs also increased but one can learn from their business strategies.

Online Sales

If you enjoy artistic talents, sell your creations on sites such as Etsy, eBay, or even Amazon. The number of online sales continues to escalate, and if you can supplement your income from these sources, go for it! An acquaintance received a one thousand dollar mechanic bill. She gathered unnecessary things from around the house and sold these treasures for about $800 on eBay. The time required listing and shipping the items, and the fees charged, were minimal compared to the relief of being able to pay her bill. Another friend has an acquaintance with a nose for fashion. The acquaintance scours stores and buys clothing, and then my friend lists them on eBay and ships them. She keeps 30 percent of the sales price for her effort. Another friend buys stoves on Craigslist in the off-season. Oftentimes, people move into a home and want to dispose of the indoor wood-burning stoves. He buys them, paints them, and then resells them when the weather changes and demand is high. He tries to collect the stovepipes when possible, as they can be extremely expensive. He also looks for EPA-approved stoves when possible. He makes a tidy sum.

Timber Job

This can cover the gamut from employment with a timber company to special harvesting of trees for specific uses, to selective forestry work for tree health, to selling firewood. Where we live, a cord of dried firewood (soft) sells for approximately $250. Permits to cut wood from state and national forests and timber company holdings cost approximately $25. If you already own a chainsaw and have a little time, it is not a bad return on investment.

Fishing/Hunting Guides

In some states, you must hire a guide if you are a nonresident intending to hunt big game. Tourists usually travel without boats and safety equipment, so it can be easier for them to go with someone already outfitted with gear. Local hunters and fishers also know the "best" spots and can make a living taking others out to where the hunting and fishing is generally reliable.

Sales

How about converting the empty storefront in town into a shop selling local wares? If regional artists, woodworkers, and food preservers rent a space for a small price, you can collaborate to draw in tourists. This might also help other local shops and restaurants. Local bands get exposure and more opportunities to play and sell their music. Maybe the store is only open a few days a week or has a co-op structure where everyone watches the store one day a month, being open every weekend, but no more. The owner of the building might charge rock-bottom rental rates so he/she no longer has to pay to heat and maintain the building. A win-win for renter and owner. When you live in the country, you often benefit by connecting with your community, play to its strengths, add value, and think asymmetrically.

Team work

Miscellaneous

Our local community has an online forum where people post tasks or jobs they want done. These range from painting, weeding, mowing, fence building, limbing and cutting, wood stacking, window washing, house cleaning, to field and orchard work. Growing up, I worked in the fields, and I did the same after college when I needed employment for a few weeks. There were no temporary agencies at the time, but I needed some money, so did what I needed to do. Another moneymaking scheme is snow dependent. When I was younger, I drove over a particular mountain pass regularly. In my little two-wheel drive sedan, in the winter I would inevitably pull over to put chains on my tires. Almost every time, someone approached me and offered to put them on for $20 to $25. I did not have extra money, so I became extremely proficient at putting them on myself — under ten minutes and I was on my way. Since help was often available, I presumed the people who stopped found enough takers to make some extra money when the snow fell.

https://goo.gl/ZT1xz7

A Final Thought: You Can Homestead

I once read a book advising that we should move toward what we want instead of away from what we feared. We met a young couple at a park when Jack introduced us. He had been playing with their children. Talking to them, we realized we all shared the common goal of homesteading. They lived in a bustling suburb of a big city, in a rented townhouse, on a busy road, with little yard, and the husband was poorly paid. Despite their circumstances, and what first appeared to be an unachievable goal, they took steps to recreate their lives. This couple began by saving loose change, growing herbs and vegetables in pots on their patios, changing their diet toward more whole foods, and homeschooling their children. While he worked and she taught, they endeavored toward their goal, saving, scrimping, and making the necessary sacrifices to buy a rural property. Recently, they bought a house on a quarter-acre and have already started gardening and acquired chickens and goats. He built a chicken coop. She ferments, cooks, and cans. They planted fruit trees and bushes this spring. Their tenacity and hard work inspires us.

Modern homesteading does not mean 600 acres in the middle of nowhere. If you are interested in homesteading, start today. Plant a small garden, bake some bread, fix the old tools needing repair, and spend time actively engaged with your family. These steps are not only for hard-core homesteaders, they are for everyone and can be implemented in urban, suburban, and small-town settings. Modern homesteading means doing what you can, with what you have, where you are. This is modern homesteading.

https://goo.gl/pJOXpj

Index:

Photo Credits:

Photo Credits: T-top, B-bottom, L-left, R-right, C-Center

Alan M. Thornton Productions: Cover, p 1, p 2-3, p 4, p 12, p 19, p 21, p 29, p 30, p 31 (3), p 32, p 84, p 85 (B), p 86, p 87, p 97 (back cover), p 104, p 105 C, p 106, p 107, p 108, p 120 B, p 147, p 154, p 155 (4), p 157 (3), p 158, p 160, p 163, p 178, p 179 (4), p 181 (3), p 183 R(3), p 184, p 185 (2), p 187, p 188 (2), p 192, p 194

Zen Todd Photographers: p 34

Astrid Melton: p 31 RC

Jean Collins: p 61, p 66

Tony Collins: p 65, p 67

Patricia Castillo: p 64

Authors: p 8, p 10, p 14, p 15, p 16, p 17, p 20 (3), p 22, p 23, p 25, p 33, p 37, p 38, p 39, p 41, p 42, p 43, p 45, p 46, p 47, p 48, p 51 B, p 53, p 54, p 56, p 57 (3), p 58, p 59, p 61, p 62, p 65, p 66, p 67, p 72, p 75, p 77, p 79, p 80, p 81, p 83, p 88, p 89, p 90, p 91, p 94, p 95, p 99, p 101, p 105 CR, p 109, p 110, p 111, p 112, p 113, p 116 (2), p 117, p 120T, p 121, p 123, p 128, p 129, p 131, p 132, p 133, p 135, p 136, p 138, p 139, p 145, p 148 (2), p 150, p 153, p 159, p 161, p 162, p 164, p 165, p 168, p 169, p 171, p 175, p 186, p 189, p 190, p 193, p 195, p 197, p 200, p 205, p 206

Shutterstock.com: p 5, p 13, p 26, p 27, p 35, p 40, p 49, p 50, p 51 (3)R, p. 52, p 55, p 68, p 71, p 73, p 74, p 76, p 78, p 85 T (2), p 92, p 100, p 102, p 105 T & B, p 114-115, p 124, p 125 (4), p 126, p 137, p 141, p 143, p 152, p 183 C, p 196, p 207

istock.com: p 70 (2), p 202

Dreamstime.com: pg 85 C

Flickr.com/dianabog: p 119, p 170